Nature in Downland

W. H. Hudson

DODO PRESS

Nature in Downland

W. H. Hudson [1841-1922]

WITH A NOTE BY EDWARD GARNETT [1868-1937]

1900

CONTENTS

CHAPTER VII

SHEPHERDS AND WHEATEARS

The shepherd's altered condition—His loss of the wheatear harvest—The passion for wheatears—Arrival of the birds on the downs—"Our ortolan"—Coops—The wheatear's habits—Sensitiveness to rain—Hurdis and the "pence of ransom"—A great dame collecting wheat-ears—John Dudeney's recollections—Shepherds cease taking wheatears—Probable reason—How the birds are now obtained—Bird-catchers, poulterers, and fanners—The law must be enforced—Lark-eating.

CHAPTER VIII

SILENCE AND MUSIC

The art of music—Natural music—Sussex voices—A pretty girl with a musical voice—Singing of the peasants—Dr. Burton on Sussex singing—Primitive singing—A shepherdess and her cries—The Sussex sheep-dog's temper—Silence of the hills—Bird music of the downs—Common bunting—Linnet—Stonechat—Whinchat—-The distance which sound travels—Experience with tramps—Singing of skylarks—Effects which cannot be expressed.

CHAPTER IX

SUMMER HEAT

When the downs are most enjoyable—July in the wooded lowland—The bliss of summer—Children's delight in heat—Misery of cold—Piers Plowman—Langland's philosophy—The happiest man in Sussex—A protection from the sun—Heat not oppressive on the hills—Birds on Mount Harry—A cup of cold water—Drawing water in a hat—Advantages of a tweed hat—An unsympathetic woman—Beauty of kindness.

CHAPTER X

SWALLOWS AND CHURCHES

Abundance of swallows in downland villages—The swallows' bat-like faculty—Old house at Ditchling—Church owls and Ditchling

Church—Shingled spires—Pleasure of finding churches open—A strange memorial in a downland church—A nap in West Firle churchyard—Slow-worms in churchyards—Increase of swallows at Ditchling—House-martins on telegraph wires—The telegraph a benefit to birds—Telegraph poles in the landscape—Sound of telegraph wires—A cockney's bird-lore—A Sussex man on swifts—Swifts at Seaford—A Somerset bird-boy's strange story.

CHAPTER XI

AUTUMN

Suddenness of the change from summer to autumn on the downs—Birds in autumn—Meadow-pipits—Shore birds on the hills—September flowers—Remnant of insect-life—Effect of rough weather—Effect on the mind of the cessation of life—Man's long life—An immortal surveying the insect tribes of human kind—The prospect from the hills—Pleasure of walking.

CHAPTER XII

WEST OF THE ADUR

Autumn on the west downs—Abundance of birds—Village of Cocking—Drayton's *Polyolbion*—A company of magpies; their inconsequent behaviour—Magpie and domestic pigeon—Story of a pet magpie—Blackberries on the downs—Elderberries—Yews at Kingly Bottom—A tradition—Yew-berries and the missel-thrushes' orgy—Hawthorn wood—Charm of the thorn-tree—Beeches on the west downs—Effect of trees on the South Downs—Gilpin's strictures answered—Characteristic trees and bushes—Juniper—A curious effect—Character of the juniper tree.

CHAPTER XIII

THE MARITIME DISTRICT

The autumnal movement of birds—Linnets on the downs—Birds wintering in the maritime district—Character of the district—Birdham—Rooks and starlings—Skylarks and finches—Dunnock and wren—Pewits on the Cuckmere—Pewit's hatred of the rook—Pewit's wing-exercises—Pewits in flocks—Black-headed gulls—Charm of the maritime district—Gloomy weather—Missel-thrush:

his temper, habits, and song—The spire of Chichester Cathedral: its aesthetic value in the landscape.

A NOTE ON HUDSON'S LITERARY ART

I

In a letter to me, of December 10, 1916, Hudson, speaking of the appreciative reviews of the American edition of Green Mansions, adds, "Not a gleam of the critical faculty in anything! " And, on turning over the few critical obituary notices that appeared after Hudson's death, one felt a certain disappointment. Excluding the papers written by Mr. H. J. Massingham [Footnote: *The Nation*, August 26, 1922.] and Mr. John Galsworthy [Footnote: *The Evening Post*, New York, September 16, 1922.] there was nothing said in point of insight that approached the sharp felicity of Mr. Conrad's tribute: "You can't tell how this fellow gets his effects. He writes as the grass grows. " Our professional literary guides spoke in terms eulogistically vague or magisterial. Mr. J. C. Squire's estimate of Hudson's creative achievement [Footnote: *The Observer*, August 20, 1922.] certainly had a judicial ring. But, without the taste for Hudson's quality, a critical appraisement suggests a game of blind man's buff. Let me quote a passage:

For Mr. Hudson's English very seldom failed. The style being the man, the style had limitations. The man's love for nature burned with a steady and equable radiance; he drank, if you like, perpetually from that fountain, but never to intoxication. He seldom felt like rhapsodising: he never came near swooning with sesthetic delight nor was taken up in religious exaltation. Spirit and sense were always awake in him, but temperate in their enjoyments. Add his general lack of humour and his proclivity towards retrospection and regret, and you get naturally something like a dead-level of writing. For a man who wrote so much and so well he produced very few "memorable pages. " The anthologists who hunt for purple passages of prose will find that he constantly baffles them; one page is so like another, and when they like two sentences they will not want the third, which will very likely change the subject. He had the defects of his qualities and the qualities of his defects. He wrote carefully; his constructions are clear and his epithets accurate. Beyond that the deliberate artificer did not often go. He was preoccupied with his matter; he wrote about certain things in a certain mood, and took no pains to play upon the eyes and ears of his readers. One looks through his style as through glass—slightly-tinted glass—at the objects behind it; and his loveliest passages as a rule are simply those in which the loveliest objects are mentioned.

The tone here is of magisterial finality, but these restricted encomiums do not seem to have got the range either of Hudson's spirit, or of his masterpieces, or of his literary art. They cannot be stretched to apply, on the one hand, to *Idle Days in Patagonia, Nature in Downland, Hampshire Days, A Shepherd's*

Life, or, on the other, to *The Purple Land, El Ombu, Green Mansions*. Mr. A. Glutton Brock, in his moving tribute to Hudson, [Footnote: *Times Literary Supplement*, August 24, 1922.] comprehends, indeed, what Mr. Squire failed to grasp, the passionate depth of Hudson's nature, the breadth of his outlook and its spiritual beauty, as when he writes: "He seemed to be of no particular age and of no sex, but rather a wonderful experiencing spirit, at once impartial and passionate, giving out beauty like the sea under a sunset and heightening it by deep and calm reflection. " But when he discusses Hudson's style Mr. Brock has nothing to say but the following:

He practised no vulgar arts, and, at the same time, there was nothing in his style to tickle those absurd people who read books for their style. You can read Mr. Conrad and feel that you are doing something remarkable, that you are enjoying what the mob would not understand; but anyone can understand Hudson. There is nothing strange in his choice of words or in the turn of his sentences. Many of them, taken by themselves, have no character; they might even seem loose and vague and commonplace. He had no literary sense of the associations of words, and could say that his forest heroine in Green Mansions had a piquant expression. Perhaps because of a youth spent in South America and without literary intercourse, he wrote always like a provincial without regard for the fashions of his own time. You might think, indeed, from his style, though not from his matter, that he was one of these Victorians who had the power of writing badly so well. Like them, he had no professional arts, and never tried to make a sharp distinction between the written and the spoken word. He was as incapable of writing as of talking for effect; and quick popularity comes to those who, whether vulgarly or preciously, do write for effect.

In these remarks the critic has thrown a wide net round the "naturalness" of Hudson's style, and has landed a draught of half-truths. He has noted, justly, that Hudson's style is unequal, at times loose, and that occasionally it lapses by infelicities of phrasing. [Footnote: In saying that Hudson wrote in *Green Mansions* that the heroine had "a piquant expression, " Mr. Brock's memory seems to have misled him. What Hudson wrote was "a bright, piquant face, " p. 83.] But as to the high felicity of Hudson's style and art in his masterpieces, Mr. Brock is silent; and what can we make of his strange assertion that "Hudson had no literary sense of the association of words"? One thinks of the literary magic, of the haunting rhythms of *El Ombu*, where each word is inevitable. One thinks—but to say more is superfluous: let the reader examine for himself any score of pages in *Nature in Downland*.

It is interesting to turn from the professional critics to one of Hudson's fellow-craftsmen, Mr. Galsworthy, and mark his verdict: "As simple narrator Hudson is well-nigh unsurpassed; as a stylist he has few if any literary rivals.... The very simplicity and intimacy of his prose, this singular faculty of giving to his readers thought and feeling free from the barriers of style, hides from the reader, as it were, the greatness of that achievement. " The apparent contradiction here, " a stylist... who communicates thought and feeling free from the barriers of style, " is, in fact, a final tribute to Hudson's quality.

II

Let us come to particulars. We must remember that Hudson wrote more than twenty volumes, and that his nature books, no less than his romances, have, each, their own character. His style is not of one kind but of great variety. Further, the quality of Hudson's style varies in degree as his object is (a) to record and comment on the facts he has observed, and (b) to infect us with his own emotions and his aesthetic delight in the spectacle of nature's life. In a book, a chapter or a page he may rise from the comparatively low level of imparting knowledge to the high altitude of poetry sublimated in exquisite prose. Thus in *The Naturalist in La Plata* (1892), which is addressed primarily to natural history students, he appeals largely to intellectual interest and little to our aesthetic sense. His style here is plain, direct and a little bald, but quite sufficing for his purpose. But in the nature book that followed, *Idle Days in Patagonia* (1893), one of Hudson's objects was to mirror the strange, brooding solitariness of primitive Patagonia and its atavistic effect on the mind and senses. His prose has a masculine directness and force, a distinctive clarity and gravity, which, in certain chapters, as in that entitled "The War with Nature, " rises to high eloquence. One feels often in its resonance traces of a Spanish strain. If "the anthologists who hunt for purple passages of prose" find only "a dead level of writing" therein, or in such descriptions as that of the night spent by Hudson, when disabled, in the cabin (Chapter II.), or that of the wounded Magellanic eagle owl (Chapter XII.), or that of the strange fascination of the grey, bleak waste of the Rio Negro (Chapter XIII.), then their sense of literary style must either be atrophied or hypertophied. If Hudson's nature book *Birds in London* (1898) produced few memorable passages it is because he is recording careful observation of a bird census, conducted in the distasteful environment of the sooty metropolis. His aversion from that "old melancholy scene, " when both he and the birds, "the few metropolitan species, " were cut off from the liberating joy of sun and wind over marsh and heath and hillsides and forest glades and shining rivers, is felt in the book's lack of emotional beauty. The "natural style" here grows tame, chilled by the dull London parks and squares. But what a change in spirit, in power, in shining loveliness of diction is wrought two years later in Hudson's style in *Nature in Downland* (1900)! Though in the matter of natural history others of the nature books are more original, this is the finest and most finished in literary art. The spirit, the character, the natural features of the South Downs, of its soil, plant and bird life, human story and changing atmosphere, are caught by him with exquisite freshness and ease. What is the literary method by which he secures so perfect a mirage? The introductory chapter answers this question. It is in the nature of an overture. First we see the August sky from Kingston Hill, the vast void blue sky with no mist or cloud in it; and in the burning sun and wind thousands upon thousands of balls of silvery thistle-down are flying away from the untilled, unenclosed downs up into the infinite azure. And this sensation of aerial space, of light and heat, of wind-swept slopes and hollows, so characteristic of the great chalk hills, is driven deeper by an intimate memory of the South American pampa. A feeling of the past, of days and nights spent in another very similar scene in a vaster continent, is called in to lighten and spiritualise the impression and liberate us from, the present. All nature to Hudson's sense is one and infinite, there beyond the seas, and here in this rolling downland with its vista of the wooded Sussex weald lying beneath, and its glimpse of the grey glistening ocean. Then, by a transition to the men of Sussex, Hudson further expands our mental vision by transporting us back a century to the birthplace of Hurdis, the author of *The Favorite Village*, the Vicar of Bishopstone; and then follows a lovely passage in which

Hudson describes his own visit to "the tiniest and most characteristic downland village" and the beautiful sight that his eyes rested on as he sat at service in the little church and gazed through the open side-door at the round yellow hill and blue sky and a white calf standing motionless, "like a calf hewn out of a block of purest white chalk, " in the green meadow in brilliant sunlight. Hurdis and his fellow-Sussex writers recall Richard Jefferies and his last sad days at Goring, and, characteristically, Hudson blends his sorrowful musings on Jefferies' premature death with "a mysterious adventure" which he himself had, on coming to Goring, with "a poor outcast and wanderer" who had the Jefferies countenance. [Footnote: I may note here that on first reading this passage I took Hudson warmly to task for some of his words on Jefferies, and Hudson said he would alter them later. But the whole passage is so imbued with Hudson's feeling that now I would not wish a word away.] The chapter ends with a description of an early morning hour spent by Hudson in watching a grey plover and ringed dotterels on their feeding-ground on Goring Beach, while he talked with an old carter Whose horse was eating ribbon seaweed. But again the thought of Jefferies' end conies, "and deep beneath my happiness was an ineffable sadness. " Now this lament for a man "who was prematurely torn away from the green world he worshipped" is like a low chord which reverberates in our consciousness, a chord struck to contrast with the bright silvery notes of the morning theme. This introductory chapter may appear simple, but the crystalline purity of its style, like clear sea-water in a weed-fringed reef, holds a profusion of tones and shadows. It contains the subtle essence of Hudson's personality. But its very quietness and sureness, its grace and gravity, may deceive the sophisticated. "His loveliest passages as a rule are simply those in which the loveliest objects are mentioned, " says the critic naively. No. They are those passages inspired by Hudson's spirit when delighting most in nature's life and moved most to purest beauty of feeling. For examples of Hudson's variety of mood and tone let the reader compare with the introductory chapter the one on Chichester. Here is Hudson, the pure artist, rejoicing in giving rein to his loathing for the besotted god worshipped by the followers of Bung, "the men with soulless bloated faces and watery eyes. " I do not know in all literature a more powerful diatribe addressed to the soul of a town than in these amazing pages on a decaying, mouldy, rotting-down moral atmosphere, or a more burning fury against soulless stupidity than in the description of the tortured white owl. Let the reader turn for pleasure and relief back to the two preceding chapters, XII. "West of the Adur, " and XIII. "The Maritime District, " and note how the character of the multiplicity of features and aspects and form of living nature has been seized by Hudson with equal fidelity and zest. The pages on the mischief-loving magpies (pp. 206-207), the little story of the poor family and the stolen sovereign, on the following page, the account of the missel-thrushes' orgies in Kingly Bottom, the sketch of the character of the hawthorns and junipers; and the whole passage on the fascination of gloomy dark autumn weather in the maritime district (Chapter XIII.)—how beautifully do these descriptions contrast with the spiritual chiaroscuro of Chapters VIII. and IX., "Silence and Music" and "Summer Heat. " These last two chapters, especially, exhaling the breath of summer, have the effect of living poetry. The aesthetic charm of every chapter in turn, and of the book as a whole, lies indeed in the cunning diversity of pattern that Hudson weaves, a pattern that enmeshes Nature's variability and elusiveness, her mutability and fecundity, a pattern of blended tones and glowing colours. And the cunning diversity of patterns is secured by Hudson's many glancing, allusive, yet detailed strokes, by his genius for swift observation, by his far-ranging knowledge, his human curiosity, his freshness of emotion, his deep passion and spiritual tenderness, all directed by his aesthetic faculty. The art is instinctive. He wrote, indeed, "as the grass grows, " and this is precisely why, as Mr. Galsworthy declares, "the very freshness and intimacy of Hudson's prose... hides from its reader, as it were, the greatness of that achievement. "

EDWARD GARNETT.

CHAPTER I

THISTLE-DOWN

On Kingston Hill—View from the hill—A day of thistle-down—A memory of the pampas—Down of the dwarf thistle—First sight and pleasant memories of the downs—Resolution to write a book—Jennings' *Rambles*—Sussex in literature—Less favoured than other counties—Minor poets—Hurdis—*The Favorite Village*—In Bishopstone church—Richard Jefferies —Birds on the beach at Goring—Horses eating sea-weed.

On one of the hottest days in August of this exceptionally hot year of 1899, I spent a good many hours on the top of Kingston Hill, near Lewes. There are clear mornings, especially in the autumn months, when magnificent views of the surrounding country can be had from the flat top of that very long hill. Usually on hot summer days the prospect, with the sea of downland and the grey glinting ocean beyond on one side, the immense expanse of the wooded Sussex weald on the other, is covered with a blue obscuring haze, and this hot, windy August day was no exception. The wind, moreover, was so violent that all winged life, whether of bird or insect, had been driven into hiding and such scanty shade as existed; it was a labour even to walk against the wind. In spite of these drawbacks, and of the everywhere brown parched aspect of nature, I had here some hours of rare pleasure, felt all the more because it had not been looked for.

Kingston Hill is not one of the dome-shaped downs, where when not on the very summit you are on a slope: the top forms a level plateau or tableland of considerable extent, covered with a thick turf and occasional patches of furze, with some bramble and elder bushes. After aimlessly wandering about over this high plain for some time I went to a spot where the hill sloped away toward the valley of the Ouse. Beyond the vast sweep of parched ground beneath me, green meadows and trees were visible, with scattered village and farm houses, and the two small churches of Iford and Kingston vaguely seen in the haze.

Here, sitting on the dry grass with my face to the wind, I spent two or three hours in gazing at the thistle-down. It is a rare thing to see it as I had it before me that day; the sight of it was a surprise, and I gave myself up to the pleasure of it, wishing for no better thing. It was not only that the sight was beautiful, but the scene was vividly reminiscent of long-gone summer days associated in memory with the silvery thistle-down. The wide extent of unenclosed and untilled earth, its sunburnt colour and its solitariness, when no person was in sight; the vast void blue sky, with no mist nor cloud on it; the burning sun and wind, and the sight of thousands upon thousands of balls or stars of down, reminded me of old days on horseback on the open pampa—an illimitable waste of rust-red thistles, and the sky above covered with its million floating flecks of white.

But the South American thistle-down, both of the giant thistle and the cardoon with its huge flower-heads, was much larger and whiter and infinitely more abundant. By day the air seemed full of it, and I remember that when out with my brother we often enjoyed seeing it at night. After a day or days of wind it would be found in immense masses in the sheltered hollows, or among the tall standing stalks of the dry plants. These masses gleamed with a strange whiteness in the dark, and it used to please us to gallop our horses through them. Horses are nervous, unintelligent creatures, liable to take fright at the most familiar objects, and our animals would sometimes be in terror at finding themselves plunged breast-deep into this unsubstantial whiteness, that moved with them and covered them as with a cloud.

The smaller, more fragile English thistle-down, in so few places abundant enough to appear as an element in the scene, is beautiful too, and its beauty is, I am inclined to think, all the greater because of its colour. Seen against the deep greens and browns of the vegetation in late summer it appears white, but compared with a white feather or white flower we see that it is silvery, with a faint yellow or brown tinge, lighter but a little like the brown tinge in the glistening transparent wings of some dragon-flies and other insects.

The down on that August day was of the dwarf thistle, which has an almost stemless flower, and appears as a purple disc on the turf. It is the most common species, universal on the sheep-walks: so abundant was it this year that as you walked about the brown and yellow turf appeared everywhere flecked with silvery white—a patch of white for every square yard of ground in some places—of the dry flower with its mass of down spread around it. Thus it was that sitting on the hill, gazing over the wide slope before me, I became sensible of the way in which ball after ball rose up from the ground to fly towards and past me. It was as if these slight silvery objects were springing spontaneously into existence, as the heat opened and the wind lifted and bore them away. All round me, and as far off as such slight gauzy objects could be seen, they were springing up from the grass in this way in hundreds and thousands. Looking long and steadily at them —their birth and their flight—one could fancy that they were living things of delicate aerial forms that had existed for a period hidden and unsuspected among the matted roots of the turf, until their time had come to rise like winged ants from the soil and float on the air.

When, lying on my back, I gazed up into the blue sky, the air as far as I could see was still peopled with the flying down; and beyond all that was visible to the naked eye, far from the earth still more down was revealed by my glasses—innumerable, faintly-seen silvery stars moving athwart the immeasurable blue expanse of heaven.

Somehow, looking back at that day of abundant thistle-down, the best day of its kind that I have experienced in England, I find that it is not only a pleasant memory, but also exists as a symbol of all my days on the South Downs. For they can all be shortened in the mind to one day, marked with a thousand scenes and events, beginning with my first sight from a distance of these round treeless hills that were strange to me. Treeless they were, and if not actually repelling, as indeed some have found them, they were at all events uninviting in their naked barren aspect. No sooner had I begun to walk on and to know and grow intimate with them than I found they had a thousand unimagined pleasures, springing up in my way like those silvery stars of down on Kingston Hill—a pleasure for every day and every hour, and for every step, since it was a delight simply to walk on that elastic turf and to breathe that pure air.

But for all my pleasure and interest in the district, I had no faintest thought of a book about it. Why, indeed, should anyone dream of a book about this range of hills, so near to the metropolis, its sea coast and coast towns the favourite haunt of hundreds of thousands of annual visitors; every hill in the range, and every species of wild bird and mammal and insect and flower, known to everyone? Without inquiry I took it that there were books and books about the South Downs, as there are about every place on earth and every earthly thing; and that I did not know them because I had not looked for them, and they had never by chance come in my way. It thus happened that in all my rambles in downland, with no motive but pleasure and health, I did only that which it is customary for me to do in all places where I may happen to be—namely, to note down every interesting fact I came across in my field naturalist's journal. Now all at once "something has come into my mind"—to wit, a little book exclusively about these hills, in which I shall be able to incorporate a good number of observations which would otherwise be wasted. But I do not say like downright old Ben Jonson that it "must and shall" be written, whether far removed from the wolf's black jaw and the other objectionable animal's hoof or not. For it will be, I imagine, a small unimportant book, not entertaining enough for those who read for pleasure only, nor sufficiently scientific and crammed with facts for readers who thirst after knowledge.

Now I am beginning to find out that there does not appear to be any book about the South Downs, although that district certainly is and has always been regarded as one of England's "observables. " It is true that a portion of Louis Jennings' *Rambles Among the Hills* treats of the Sussex range, and is excellent reading; but this little work does not satisfy me, since the author misses that which to many of us is the most interesting part of the subject—namely, the wild life of the district. His libellous remarks on that worthy little beast, the mole, are proof that he is no naturalist, and could not touch on such subjects without going astray. Curiously enough, Sussex, or any part of it, can hardly be said to exist in literature; or if it has any place there and in our hearts it is a mean one, far, far below that of most counties. Let me, however, say in parentheses that I am not a great reader, and know few books, that on this subject I therefore speak as a fool, or, at all events, an ignorant person. But so far as I know, this county, so near to the metropolis, so important geographically with its long coast line of over seventy miles on the Channel, the "threshold of England, " as it has been called, the landing-place of the Conqueror and eternal grave of Saxon dominion, has produced no genius to stamp its lineaments on our minds. The Sussexian, who cares to make the boast, may indeed claim that his county has given as great names as any other to poetic and dramatic literature— Shelley, Collins, Otway, Fletcher. But Sussex was nothing to these writers, and they are nothing to Sussex. Their connection with their native place was slight; its scenery never entered into their souls to give a special colour to their lives and life-work. How differently other counties have fared in this respect! Who does not know a hundred, a thousand, places in England, as well as he knows his own home, though he may never have seen them? One has but to let one's thoughts fly hither and thither at random over the face of the country. The whole rude coast of Cornwall, where we must have lived long years in the roar of the sea, is as well known to us as the cliff at Dover and the enduring image of the suspended samphire-gatherer. What a strange significance there is in the names of many places in the south-west and western counties —Dorset, Devon, and Somerset! How many rivers we know, and how many hill-ranges all over the land, from the Quantocks to the Cheviots! But even the glorious hills and lakes and forests have not painted themselves more vividly on our minds than the featureless flats, the low shores and saltings, the wide moors; the Essex marshes with the tragic figures of Rebow and Gloria; the lonely heath by Poole water, where we have listened by night and day to the mysterious voices of the wind; and the Lincolnshire fen-land, over whose desolate expanse, shimmering in the summer heat, Mariana gazed each day in vain and said despondingly, "He cometh not! " Hills, valleys, wolds, dales, plains, marshes, rivers, lakes, moors, heaths, woods, towns, villages, are in this way known familiarly to us all over the land; but the county of Sussex is not included in this spiritual geography.

From the writers of genius who have made so much of the scenery of England familiar to us all, to those literary South Saxons who have stayed at home and written something, little or much, about their native land—Hayley, William Hay, Charlotte Smith, Parsons, Hurdis, with a few more of even less account—is indeed a tremendous descent. These are now forgotten, and their works will never come back; for though important in their own day, they were, viewed at this distance, little people who could have no place with the immortals. But I do not despise them on that account; being of that tribe myself, I have a kindly feeling for little people, not for the living only, who write in the modern fashion and are by some thought great, but also for those who have been long dead, whose fame has withered and wasted in the grave. And for the last of the few singers I have mentioned I cherish a very special regard, and should now like to tell how the forgotten name of Hurdis came by chance to be associated in my mind with the South Downs.

When I was a youth a very long time ago, in a distant land, poetry about nature had a peculiar fascination for me; but it was hard to find, and I fed mostly (when I got anything to eat) on what would now be regarded as mere dry husks. A battered old volume of Shenstone was one of the three or four poetical works I possessed. In a book of elegant extracts, in verse and prose, I came upon some passages from Hurdis—his *Village Curate*—which greatly delighted me; and now in another world, and after a thousand years, as it seems, I am surprised to find that they still live in memory. I will even venture to quote some lines of the favourite passages:

It was my admiration
To view the structure of that little work,
A bird's nest—mark it well, within, without;
No tool had he that wrought, no knife to cut,
No rail to fix, no bodkin to insert,
No glue to join: his little beak was all:
And yet how neatly finished! What nice hand,
With every implement and means of art,
And twenty years' apprenticeship to boot,
Could make me such another? Fondly then
We boast of excellence, whose noblest skill
Instinctive genius foils!

It was not strange that these lines pleased me, for I was myself then a diligent seeker and great admirer of little birds' nestles; they were pretty objects to look at, and there was, moreover, a mystery about them which made them differ from all other things. For though so admirably fashioned—whether attached to slender swaying reeds and rushes, or placed down among the grasses, or on wood, or high among the clustering leaves on trees—as to seem a natural growth, with their gem-like pearly and speckled eggs, many-coloured, resting in them like bright polished seeds in an opening capsule, yet it was not so; they had not been produced by Nature like leaf and flower and fruit, but were artificial basket-houses built with much labour, with many selected materials gathered in many places, by the little winged men and women called birds.

The other remembered passage, too long to quote in full, concludes with these excellent lines:

Give to repose the solemn hour she claims,
And from the forehead of the morning steal
The sweet occasion. Oh, there is a charm
Which morning has, that gives the brow of age
A smack of youth, and makes the lips of youth
Shed perfumes exquisite.

Nothing more did I learn of Hurdis until quite recently, after it had occurred to me to write this book, when at the Brighton Library, in looking through a collection of works, mostly rubbish, on local subjects, I came upon a long poem entitled *The Favorite Village*, by the Rev. James Hurdis—a thin quarto bound in calf in the old style, on coarse bluey-grey paper, "Printed at the Author's own Press, Bishopstone, Sussex, 1800. " This was to me a delightful discovery, not only on account of the old memories I have mentioned, but because the poem had the South Downs for its subject; also because Bishopstone, the "favorite village, " the author's birthplace and where in after life he was vicar, was well known to me, although I had not yet been in its church. After reading the work two or three times, I am compelled to say that it is very bad poetry, reminding one, in its prosy diction and occasional rhetorical outbursts, now of *The Task* and now of *The Seasons*. In all the mass of descriptive matter about the downs I am unable to find a passage worth quoting. In spite of my disappointment, when Sunday came I went to Bishopstone with a new and lively interest, and saw that small pretty village among the downs near Newhaven in its brightest and best aspect. It was early August; the corn was all cut and most of it carried, and the round treeless hills were yellow in that brilliant morning sunshine —straw-yellow against the pure ethereal blue of heaven. And in a hollow among the great hills nestled Bishopstone, out of sight but not out of hearing of the sea, when its "accents disconsolate" sound afar in the silence of the night—the tiniest and the most characteristic of the downland villages. The few houses, cottages, and farm buildings, each one unlike all the others, its own character stamped upon it, but all alike rich in the ornament of yellow, orange, grey and rust-red lichen stains, were picturesquely grouped about the small ancient flint church; and there was shade of beech and elm, and the trees were ancient-looking too, and tempest-beaten, like most others in this treeless land.

I was so fortunate as to have a seat near the middle of the church, abreast of the side door which stood wide open admitting the summer light and warmth and out-door sounds; so that while following the service I could let my eyes rest on the landscape. That was a beautiful picture I had to look at, with the doorway for frame; a round yellow hill and the blue sky beyond, and between the hill and the church a green meadow, low outhouse and fences, and a small paddock or enclosure with rooks and daws and small birds coming and going. And by-and-by, into that green enclosure came a white calf, and remained there for some time, standing motionless, in the centre of the picture. The brilliant sunlight made it luminous, and it was like a calf hewn out of a block of purest white chalk. I did not keep my eyes constantly on it; and after an interval, on looking again I found that it was gone, and that two red calves had taken its place. These were moving about cropping the grass, while several starlings were searching for grubs close to them. But these red animals were not so fascinating as the white one. And all the time I was looking at that changing picture, while following the service, I was thinking of the old last-century poet who had been dear to me so long ago—so far away. The story of his life, and his writings, poor though some of them may seem to us at this day, show that his feeling for his native place was one of strange intensity, a life-long passion; and when the *Venite Laudamus Domino* filled the little church with a sudden tempest of musical sound, the thought of his dust lying close by came to my mind, and I wished that that loud noise of the living in a quiet place could wake him out of his hundred years' sleep for a brief spell, so that he might taste the summer sunshine once more, and look once more, though but for a moment, on his beloved hills and home.

Enough of Hurdis: after having been his debtor since boyhood it is satisfactory to feel that that ancient obligation has at length been discharged in full.

We may say of Sussex that its native writers have done nothing, or nothing worth doing, for it; and that no outside writers of note have come to its aid, as has happened in the case of some other counties. Had Richard Jefferies lived it would, I believe, have been different. It is true that his soul was dyed, and dyed deeply, in that North Wilts nature which he had first beheld, where his revelation came to him; but the visible world was too much for him, and his senses too well trained, to let him rest satisfied with memories; and we may see in *The Story of my Heart* and some other of his writings, that the Sussex coast country where he found a home powerfully attracted and held him. The thirteen years that have passed since his sad death would have brought his splendid powers, always progressing until the last day of his life, to their fullest maturity: perhaps, too, that strain of intense unnatural feeling, which he so strangely misinterpreted, and which in his book just named touches the borders of insanity, would have been outgrown. I am not sure that he had not outlived that phase before he died, since his latest work is decidedly of a higher quality and, even when most inspired by passion, essentially more sober than the famous *Story*. That he would eventually have written a book about the downs and the maritime district of Sussex, as good as any work we have had from him, I feel certain.

Why I said so much about forgotten Hurdis a little while back has been explained, and now a second apology seems necessary. Jefferies was much in my mind just now because by chance I happen to be writing this introductory chapter in the last house he inhabited, and where he died, in the small village of Goring, between the sea and the West Sussex downs.

A strange, I had almost said a mysterious, adventure befell me as I came hither. On a cloudy melancholy day in September I came in search of this cottage, and walking to the church by a narrow lane with a low trim wall-like hedge on either side, my thoughts were of Jefferies, who had doubtless often walked here, too, feeling the icy hand on him of one that walked invisible at his side. My mind was full of sadness, when, hearing the crunching of gravel beneath other feet than my own, I suddenly looked up, and behold, there before me stood the man himself, back on earth in the guise of a tramp! It was a most extraordinary coincidence that at such a moment I should have come face to face with this poor outcast and wanderer who had the Jefferies countenance as I knew it from portraits and descriptions. It was the long thoughtful suffering face, long straight nose, flowing brown beard, and rather large full blue eyes. I was startled at the expression, the unmistakable stamp of a misery that was anguish and near to despair and insanity. He passed me, then paused, and after a moment or two, said hesitatingly, "Can you spare a penny? " I gave him something without looking at his face again, and went on my way sorry that I had met him, for I knew that those miserable eyes would continue to haunt me.

Here, sitting in the room that was his—the author of the strange *Story*—the morning sun filling it with brightest light, the sounds he listened to coming in at the open window—the intermittent whispering of the foliage and the deeper continuous whisper of the near sea, and cries and calls of so many birds that come and go in the garden, each "deep in his day's employ"—I cannot but think of him and lament again that he was prematurely torn away from this living green world he worshipped.

Last evening when the tide began to ebb I went down by the wet shaded lane to the beach, and sat there for a long time watching a flock of half-a-dozen little ringed dotterels running about and feeding on a small patch of clean sand among the shingle. For three days these dotterels had come to the same spot at the turn of the tide, one grey plover always in their company. Evidently no one with a gun had seen and fired at this plover, and living with the small tame dotterels he had grown tame, too; and it seemed wonderful to me that this shy bird should continue quietly feeding within forty yards of where I sat, glass in hand, never tired of admiring his rarely seen figure and beautifully harmonious grey mottled plumage.

Very early this morning, on going to the beach, I found the birds back on their little feeding-ground, just uncovered by the sea; and close by, sitting on a groin, was an old man, a carter with his cart and two horses beside him, patiently waiting for the water to get a little lower before taking up a load of sand in his cart. He was a handsome old man, of the type I have so often admired on the Sussex downs, with a strong large frame, noble aquiline features, and an intelligent expression. He told me that he had seen a kingfisher flying along the coast, just over the water: its shining blue colour had startled him as it flashed by, for it was a rare sight at that spot. I had watched one, probably the same bird, two or three days before, fishing from a groin in a rough sea. The old man got down from his seat and, picking up a very big bunch of ribbon seaweed, shook out the water and sand and gave half of it to one horse and half to the other. They ate it greedily, as if it had been the most fragrant new-mown hay. I had seen New Forest ponies browsing on furze, deftly cutting off the big prickly blossoming sprays with their uncovered chisel—like teeth, and calmly chewing them up apparently without hurt to their tender mouths; but to see horses contentedly champing seaweed was new to me. Some horses liked it and some refused to eat it, he told me. It was supposed to be good for them to eat it in moderation; his own opinion was that horses that ate seaweed were stronger and kept their health better than others.

And so we talked for half an hour, standing in the glorious morning sunshine, the green withdrawing sea growing smoother by degrees, but far out we could see it still rough with big rollers, foam-crested; the little ringed dotterels and the large grey plover running about on the sand and feeding unconcerned near us; the big patient horses standing with masses of wet seaweed glistening at their feet. It was very wonderful, and I was happy and laughed with the old carter as we talked; but the thought of Jefferies, slain before his time by hateful destiny, still haunted me, and deep down beneath my happiness was an ineffable sadness.

CHAPTER II

CHARM OF THE DOWNS

Scope and limits of this work—A general description of the downs—Agreeable sensations: an inquiry into their causes—Gilbert White's speculations—The pleasures of the downs due to a variety of causes—Their shapely human-like curves—Connection between the senses of sight and touch—Effects of flowing outlines—Instinctive delight in wide horizons—The desire to fly—Effect of a series of dome-like forms—The joy of mountains.

When I stated, perhaps ignorantly, in the last chapter that nothing had been done by writers of note or of genius for Sussex, the statement did not include works of a purely scientific description. There is no lack of that kind of literature; the geology especially of the great range of chalk hills that distinguish this county, and of the Weald, has been treated at very considerable length.

I am not concerned with this aspect of the subject—the framework or skeleton of downland and the wonderful story of its creation; but only with its smooth surface from the aesthetic point of view, and with the living garment of the downs, its animal and vegetable forms, from the point of view of the lover of nature and, in a moderate degree, of the field naturalist. These impressions of the downs—of their appearance and the feelings they evoke in us—need only to be prefaced by a few sentences descriptive of the range generally.

The South Downs and the Sussex Downs, as general use will now have it, mean the same thing; strictly speaking, the name of South Downs is limited to that portion of the range which rises abruptly from the flat marsh of Pevensey, and extends from Beachy Head westward to the river Adur, a distance of twenty-six miles. The range of the South Downs proper is itself cut through by two rivers—the Cuck-mere, with the famous old village of Alfriston on its bank, and the more important Ouse, which flows by Lewes and enters the sea at Newhaven. Two other rivers cut through the Sussex range before it enters Hampshire—the Arun, with the picturesque town of Arundel on its banks, a dozen miles or so west of the Adur, and about nine miles west of the Arun the little Lavant. The whole length of the Sussex range, from Beachy Head to the western extremity of the county, is fifty-three miles.

For the first sixteen miles of its westward course from Pevensey the range keeps to the sea, forming an almost continuous white cliff to Brighton. At this point it begins to diverge gradually from the coast, until at Chichester near the west border of the county the strip of low flat land between the sea and the downs has a breadth of several miles.

On the south side of the range the hills are as a rule lowest, and slope gradually to the sea. The aspect of the downs on this side is familiar to most of us, owing to the large number of persons, probably amounting to millions annually, who visit one or other of the seaside towns and villages that extend in a chain along this part of the south coast, from Eastbourne to the Selsey peninsula, near Chichester. The hills are highest on the north side, where they rise abruptly from the flat weald, like a gigantic buttressed wall, or an earthwork reared of old by Titans. The loftiest part of the range is in the South Downs proper, where, in the neighbourhood of Lewes, east and west of that town, one may walk many miles along the crest of the hill, on a turf which makes walking a joy, and keep at a height of from 700 to 860 feet above the sea level, the ocean six or seven miles distant on one hand, the deep-green wooded flat country of the weald on the other.

West of the break caused by the river Adur, the range, on its north side, rises again to a height of about 800 feet, at Chanctonbury, and continues high to the valley of the Arun. West of that river the downs are less high, and being wooded differ in the character of their scenery from that of the great naked hills in the eastern part of the range.

I myself prefer to approach the downs on the north side, rather than walk five to seven or eight miles from the coast before getting to the highest point. The climb up the steep smooth escarpment is a good preparation, an intensifier of the pleasure to follow. Those who know the downs are all agreed that it *is* a rare pleasure to be on them. And when we have had our upward toil on a hot day, and are at length on the level plateau-like summit, on the turf; when the wind has blown us dry, and we have experienced that sense of freedom and elation which is the result of rising from a low level into a ratified atmosphere, these purely physical sens"a-tions are succeeded by a higher, more enduring pleasure, which the mind receives from the prospect disclosed. I mean the prospect of the vast round green hills extending away on either hand to the horizon. What is the secret of this peculiar pleasure? We may say off-hand that it is nothing but the instinctive delight which we have in wild nature and a wide prospect. And this is no doubt a principal element in the feeling—wild nature and a wide prospect in unenclosed country, an elastic turf under foot, and full liberty to roam whithersoever we will. There is another element resulting from the conformation of the earth's surface—the special character of the scenery. The wildness, the wide horizon and sense of liberty after the confinement of roads and fences and hedges, come first: it is the local aspect, appealing as it does to the aesthetic faculties, which makes the feeling distinctive. Thus, among mountains, on moors, and in vast desolate marshes, on iron-bound coasts, and on wide seaside flats and saltings, and on level plains, I experience this same feeling of elation, which yet differs in character in each locality, and I may be able to analyse my feelings in all or some of these cases and find out why they differ. What is to be said concerning the special quality of the South Downs—the mental flavour they impart?

I remember that Gilbert White speculated on this very question, in the often-quoted Letter LVI., where he says:

Though I have now travelled the Sussex Downs upwards of thirty years, yet I still investigate that chain of majestic mountains with fresh admiration year by year, and I think I see new beauties each time I traverse it.... For my own part, I think there is something peculiarly sweet and amusing in the shapely-figured aspect of chalk hills, in preference to those of stone, which are rugged, broken, abrupt, and shapeless. Perhaps I may be singular in my opinion... but I never contemplate these mountains without thinking I perceive somewhat analogous to growth in their gentle swellings and smooth fungus-like protuberances, their fluted sides and regular hollows and slopes, that carry at once the air of vegetative dilatation and expansion: or was there ever a time when the calcareous masses were thrown into fermentation by some adventitious moisture— were raised and leavened into shape by some plastic power, and so made to swell and heave their broad backs into the sky, so much above the less animated clay of the wild below?

"Sweet and amusing" are not words we should now use in this connection; but the description is pleasant, and the speculations, albeit fanciful, are suggestive; for it is a fact that the attractiveness of these broad hills is in a measure due to their fungus-like roundness and smoothness. But not only to these qualities, as we find when we leave the chain to look upon an isolated down: it fails to attract; the charm is not in the one but in the many. Furthermore, it is due to a combination of various causes. To begin with, we have the succession of shapely outlines; the vast protuberances and deep divisions between, suggestive of the most prominent and beautiful curves of the human figure, and of the "solemn slope of mighty limbs asleep. " That modern poet's vision of a Titanic woman reclined in everlasting slumber on the earth, her loose sweet-smelling hair lying like an old-world forest over leagues of ground; the poet himself sitting for ever, immersed in melancholy, in the shadow of her great head, has seemed a mere outcome of a morbid imagination. Here, among the downs, the picture returns to the mind with a new light, a strange grandeur; it is not a mere "flower of disease" and nothing more, but is rather a start-lingly vivid reminder that we ourselves are anthropomorphic and mythopoeic, even as our earliest progenitors were, who were earth-worshippers in an immeasurably remote past, before the heavenly powers existed.

Here, too, where the lines of the earth are most human-like, we are reminded of the philosophic doctrine that for us all nature is a secondary object of the passion of love, and that to this fact the beauty of nature is chiefly due. The scene also takes us back to the discredited Hogarthian notion concerning the origin of our idea of beauty; and at the same time of Burke's theory of the beautiful. This, too, has fallen into neglect, if not contempt, oddly enough, since it contains the germ of our modern philosophy of the beautiful. Perhaps it would not be an exaggeration to say that it contains a good deal more than the germ. Burke was assuredly right in maintaining that there exists a very close connection between the senses of sight and feeling, and in tracing the agreeable sensations arising from the contemplation of soft and smooth surfaces in this connection. To put the theory into five short words—*what we see we feel*.

When we look on a landscape, particularly when it is seen from a considerable elevation, the body goes with the mind or vision; in other words, locomotion is associated with seeing—we are there, as it were, roaming corporeally over the expanse we are gazing on. When we look at the sky, or a cloud, or the sea, the sight does not instinctively rest on it, but is satisfied with a glance; if we continue to gaze, not occupied with something in us, but seeing vividly, it is because some object or some strange or beautiful atmospheric effect excites our admiration or curiosity; or because we are artists, or sailors, or fishermen, and have an interested motive in studying water or sky. "I cannot stand all day on a naked beach watching the capricious hues of the sea, " pathetically wrote Charles Lamb from some spot on the south coast. "I would fain retire into the interior of my cage. While I gaze on the sea I want to be on it, over it, across it. There is no home for me here. " I have read that in convents and harems there is an arrangement of the windows which prevents the inmates from looking out or down upon the earth; they are constrained to look up, presumably because there is no male form, nor shadow nor reflection of one, in the void above. Those who have been fenced in from harm in this fashion must have hated the blue sky as much as Tennyson's worn-out mariners hated the dark blue wave. I have noticed that birds when perched do, even when they appear to be reposing, gaze a good deal at the sky. They are aerial, of the sky, and are accustomed to travel and dwell there with spread wings; and their fellows and enemies are there.

The sea and the sky in their ordinary aspects do not hold the attention, because we are not of them, and do not feel them, and the sensation of moving in or on them is consequently not here associated with seeing. The sight dwells with pleasure on the downs, because they are, in appearance, easy to walk upon, and in a sense are being walked upon when looked at.

Here, it may be remarked, that a surface which appears easy to the feet is also easy to the sight. The greater pleasure which we receive from flowing outlines than from those that are angular, as Herbert Spencer has pointed out, is due to the harmonious unrestrained action of the ocular muscles occupied in the perception of such outlines. On these downs, for the sight and that bodily sensation which cannot be dissociated from sight, there are no impassable chasms, no steep heights difficult to climb, nor jagged rocks and broken surfaces to impede free movement and passage.

Finally we have as another important element in our pleasure the large prospect disclosed. Why a wide horizon should have so great a fascination for us, wingless walkers on the level ground, is a curious question. It is not merely a childish delight in a novel sensation; I should rather look on it as a survival, like our fighting, hunting, and various other instincts—an inherited memory of a period when the hill—top was at the same time refuge, fortress, and tower of observation from which all hidden things stood revealed—where men, losing their fear and feeling superior to their enemies, were lifted above themselves.

One would be only too glad to believe the feeling to be different in its origin, and in a sense prophetic—like the unnecessarily large brains of primitive man, according to the Wallacian doctrine— pointing to a time when we shall be able, with the aid of perfected machinery, or better still, by means of some mysterious undeveloped faculty within us, to rise from earth and float hither and thither at will through the boundless fields of air.

Oddly enough, that desire which we all have at times for wings, or at all events for the power of flight, and which like other vague and idle promptings is capable of cultivation and of being made a real source of pleasure, most often comes to me on these great green hills. Here are no inviting woods and mysterious green shades that ask to be explored: they stand naked to the sky, and on them the mind becomes more aerial, less conscious of gravity and a too solid body. Standing on one great green hill, and looking across vast intervening hollows to other round heights and hills beyond and far away, the wish is more than a wish, and I can almost realise the sensation of being other than I am—a creature with the instinct of flight and the correlated faculty; that in a little while, when I have gazed my full and am ready to change my place, I shall lift great heron-like wings and fly with little effort to other points of view.

To come back from this digression, or flight. It is true that the extent of earth visible from the very highest downs is not really great, but with a succession of dome-like outlines extending to the horizon we have to take into account the illusion of infinite distance produced on the mind by the repetition of similar forms. The architect, in a small way, produces the same effect in his colonnades. I was once very much struck by an effect of this kind at sea, in the South Atlantic, when during perfectly calm weather there was a stupendous swell, the long vast glassy rollers succeeding one another at regular intervals. Viewed from the bridge of the steamer the ocean appeared to have increased immeasurably in extent; the horizon was no wider than before, yet it was as if I had been lifted hundreds of feet above the surface.

Those of my readers whose minds run on mountains, and the joy of mountains, may say here that, in spite of the illusion produced, the height of the downs is really so small that the pleasure arising from that cause must be comparatively very little. It is, I think, a very common error that the degree of pleasure we have in looking on a wide prospect depends on our height above the surrounding earth—in other words, that the wider the horizon the greater the pleasure. The fact is, once we have got above the world, and have an unobstructed view all round, whether the height above the surrounding country be 500 or 5000 feet, then we at once experience all that sense of freedom, triumph, and elation which the mind is capable of. This "sudden glory, " which may be ours on a very modest elevation, is the most we can hope for: we can no more get a new sensation or a larger measure of the quickly-vanishing pleasure we have enjoyed by transporting ourselves to the highest summits on the globe, than we can change a Skye terrier into an eagle by taking it three or four miles up in a balloon and throwing it out of the car.

What we do get by ascending to greater heights, to the limits of our endurance, is the mountain scenery, the new aspects of nature, which have an aesthetic value. This is the same kind of pleasure which we experience in walking or riding through a picturesque country; but the aesthetic pleasure of the mountain may actually seem more, or keener, on account of the greater novelty—the unlikeness of the scene to the more or less familiar aspects of nature on the level earth. For we live on the earth and pay but brief visits to mountain summits.

CHAPTER III

THE LIVING GARMENT

The South Downs most agreeable in the hot season—Beauty
of the bindweed—Black oxen—The old Sussex breed of
cattle—Black oxen in poetry—Suggestion for group of
statuary—Black and gold in nature—Turf of the downs—
Result of breaking up the turf—A new flora—Variety of
colonising plants—Beauty of the chance-made gardens of
the downs—Flowers in barren places—Forget-me-nots—
Viper's bugloss—Effects of blue flowers in masses—A
shepherd boy in sainfoin—Field scabious—Fertile spots—
Dropwort and heath—Harebells—Brilliant colour and
intensity of life—Minute flowers of the turf—Old Gerarde—
Eyebright: its obscure habits—The dwarf thistle.

The South Downs, in their cultivated parts, are seen at their best in
July and August, when the unreaped corn turns from green to red
gold: whether the tint be yellow or red, it strikes one as more intense
than on the lower levels. Then, too, among the ripe corn, along the
ragged fringes of the field, and close to the dusty path, the
bindweed, adorned with its delicate rose-coloured blossoms, runs
riot; and twining in and out among the dry, bright stalks, its green,
string-like wandering stem has something of the appearance of an
exceedingly attenuated tree-snake. Why is it that this most graceful
weed, seen in the wheat, invariably gives me the idea of a sentient
being delighting in its own mischievous life? It is the pretty spoilt
darling of the fields who has run away to hide in the corn, and to
peer back, with a roguish smile on its face, at every passer-by.
Perhaps the farmer is partly to blame for the fancy, for the bindweed
vexes his soul, as it will vex and hinder the reapers by-and-by; and
he abuses it just as if it had a moral sense and ears to hear, and ought
to be ashamed of itself. It pleased me to be told by a village maiden
that not bindweed, nor convolvulus, but *lilybind* was the true name
of this pretty plant.

Here one may see the corn reaped with sickles in the ancient way;
and better still, the wheat carried from the field in wains drawn by
two or three couples of great, long-horned, black oxen. One wonders
which of the three following common sights of the Sussex downs
carries us further back in time: the cluster of cottages, with church

and farm buildings, that form the village nestling in the valley, and, seen from above, appearing as a mere red spot in the prospect; the cloaked shepherd, crook in hand, standing motionless on some vast green slope, his grey, rough-haired sheep-dog resting at his feet; or the team of coal-black, long-horned oxen drawing the plough or carrying the corn.

The little rustic village in the deep dene, with its two or three hundred inhabitants, will probably outlast London, or at all events London's greatness; and the solitary shepherd with his dog at his feet will doubtless stand watching his flock on the hillside for some thousands of years to come; but these great, slow, patient oxen cannot go on dragging the plough much longer; the wonder is that they have continued to the present time. One gazes lovingly at them, and on leaving casts many a longing, lingering look behind, fearing that after a little while their place will know them no more for ever.

I have described these oxen used in farm-work on the downs as black in colour, and very nearly all of them are black; but the fact is, this variety only dates back about a century in this district, and was introduced from Wales, though for what reason no one appears to know, since the original red Sussex ox was always a "kindly and handsome" beast and a good worker. A few teams of the red oxen may still be seen among the downs, probably some of these, as on the Earl of Chichester's farm at Stanmer, being kept more for the sentiment of the thing than for any other reason. They are noble-looking animals, well-shaped, long-horned, of a deep, rich, red colour, a very much deeper red than the Devonshire cattle, but not brown. These are of the original Sussex breed, for which this county was once famous when it was undoubtedly the greatest cattle-breeding district in England. "How great on all sides is the abundance of cattle, but how strange a solitude of men! " says an old traveller, when speaking of the Sussex weald. And Arthur Young, in his famous *Tour through the Southern Counties* (1768) telling of the bad roads in this cattle-breeding district, says: "Here I had a sight, which indeed I never saw in any other part of England, namely, that going to church in a village not far from Lewes, I saw an ancient lady of very good quality drawn to church in her coach with six oxen: nor was it done but out of mere necessity, the way being so stiff and deep that no horses could go in it. " The necessity no longer exists; and the horse is rapidly taking his place even in the oxen's proper work. Down to 1834, according to Ellman, the well-known improver of the South Down sheep, almost every farmer in Sussex worked oxen as well as horses. What a change to the present time, when the few farmers who still make use of oxen tell you that even those few are not bred in the county, that Sussex is now obliged to go into other counties to get its cattle! Within the last five or six years I have seen the use of oxen given up in farms where they had always been employed, and I greatly fear that those who will walk on the downs a quarter of a century hence will see no patient team of "slow black oxen. "

It is possible that black oxen similar to those of Sussex may still be used in farm-work in some parts of Ireland: I have not penetrated far into the interior of that distant country. At all events, it seems unlikely that a Nationalist and leader of the "Celtic School, " Mr. W. B. Yeats, should have come to the most Saxon district in England to get that grand and sombre simile with which he concludes his poetic drama of *The Countess Cathleen*:

Tell them that walk upon the floor of peace
That I would die and go to her I love;
The years like great black oxen tread the world,
And God the herdsman goads them on behind,
And I am broken by their passing feet.

The black oxen figure nobly, too, in Mrs. Marriott Watson's poem, *On the Downs*, and these are our familiar Sussex beasts. I will here quote more than the necessary lines; and the reader who knows and loves the district will agree that a more perfect picture of downland in one of its many aspects was never written:

Broad and bare to the skies.
The great down country lies.
Green in the glance of the sun.
Fresh with the keen, salt air:
Screaming the gulls rise from the fresh-turned mould,
Where the round bosom of the wind-swept wold
Slopes to the valley fair.

Where the pale stubble shines with golden gleam,
The silver plough-share cleaves its hard-won way
Behind the patient team,
The slow black oxen toiling through the day:
Tireless, impassive still

From dawning dusk and chill
To twilight grey.
Far off, the pearly sheep
Along the upland steep
Following the shepherd from the wattled fold,
With tinkling bell-notes falling sweet and cold
As a stream's cadence, while a skylark sings
High in the blue with eager, outstretched wings,
Till the strong passion of his joy he told.

If unlimited wealth were mine I should be tempted to become the
owner of one of these great hills, to place upon it, as a gift to
posterity, a representation in some imperishable material of these
black cattle engaged with their human fellow-creatures in getting in
the harvest. Doubtless the people of the future would say that the
hill was never really mine to dispose of as I thought proper; but I
imagine that for their own sakes they would respect the statuary, the
memorial of a vanished time:

  Cold Pastoral!
When old age shall this generation waste,
Thou shalt remain, in midst of other woe
Than ours, a friend to man.

To begin with, a sculptor of genius would be required, a giant
among artists; and the materials would be gigantic blocks of granite
and marble—red, black, grey, and yellow. From these would be
wrought, twice or thrice the size of life, a group—a partly-loaded
waggon, drawn by three couples of great black bullocks, attended by
four or five labourers in their rough grey garments, strong men with
brown bearded faces and smooth-cheeked youths; one on the top of
the load, the others with their forks tossing up more sheaves; the
oxen holding up their horned, shaggy fronts—all but the leaders,
who have more freedom; and these would be turning aside with
lowered heads, eagerly snatching mouthfuls of yellow straw from a
sheaf fallen by chance in their way.

I have simply described what I saw in the course of my last late July
ramble on the downs; and it seemed only natural to wish to be able
to set up a copy which would remain unruined by time and weather
for at least a thousand years. The arrangement of the group as well
as the form of the creatures composing it—men and great rough-
hewn cattle—was wonderfully fine; but I also think that colour was a

principal element in the fascinating effect the spectacle produced — the contrast of those large living black masses with the shining red and gold of the wheat. How strikingly beautiful — startlingly, one might almost say, on account of its rarity — this contrast of black and gold is in nature may be seen even in so comparatively small a creature as a blackbird, perched or moving about amid the brilliant yellow foliage of a horse-chestnut or some other tree in October. Again, a large mass of yellow sunlit foliage seen against a black rain-cloud shows us the same contrast on a grand scale.

The downs are nowhere tame, but I seldom care to loiter long in their cultivated parts. It seems better to get away, even from the sight of labouring men and oxen, and of golden corn and laughing bindweed, to walk on the turf. This turf is composed of small grasses and clovers mixed with a great variety of creeping herbs, some exceedingly small. In a space of one square foot of ground, a dozen or twenty or more species of plants may be counted, and on turning up a piece of turf the innumerable fibrous interwoven roots have the appearance of cocoa-nut matting. It is indeed this thick layer of interlaced fibres that gives the turf its springiness, and makes it so delightful to walk upon. It is fragrant, too. The air, especially in the evening of a hot spring day, is full of a fresh herby smell, to which many minute aromatic plants contribute, reminding one a little of the smell of bruised ground-ivy. Or it is like the smell of a druggist's shop, blown abroad and rid of its grosser elements: the medicine smell with something subtler added — aroma and perfume combined, the wholesome fragrance of the divine Mother's green garment, and of her breath.

But all the untilled downland is not turf: there are large patches of ground, often of twenty or thirty to a hundred acres in extent, where there is no proper turf, and the vegetation is of a different character. Some of these patches have a very barren appearance, and others are covered with grass and flowers in spring, but in summer are dry and yellow or brown, when the turf all round keeps its verdure. This difference in the vegetation is not caused by a difference of soil, as one is at first apt to imagine, but to the fact that the ground of some former period has been tilled. I have looked at many patches of this kind of land, which had not been tilled for periods of from five to five-and-twenty years, and they mostly had the same character. In spring they produce a scanty crop of thin grass, rarely worth cutting, and by July it has all vanished; and the sun-baked soil has by then an exceedingly barren appearance, with its sprinkling of thistles, and a few minute creeping herbs. This kind of land, spoilt by the plough, is said by the shepherds to be "sickly"; and the grass that grows in it, little in quantity and poor in quality, they call "gratton grass. "

It has been said that if the turf is once destroyed by ploughing on the downs it never grows again. This is not absolutely true, as we may find in the old Roman earthworks, of which there are so many on the high downs, and which are now covered with as close and rich a turf as may be seen anywhere. But this is undoubtedly to go too far back. That Nature takes an unconscionably long time to remake the turf characteristic of the downs, when once it has been unmade by the plough, there is a means of knowing. It happened that in 1800, when wheat rose to the enormous price of 160 shillings, and even more, per quarter, that on the South Downs, as in many other places throughout the country, a great deal of grazing land was brought under cultivation. Much of this land, which was cultivated for a year or two, has remained untilled ever since; and we see that like the "sickly" lands that were tilled ten to twenty years ago it has not yet got a turf. But in some respects it differs from the sickly land; for although unlike the turfy downland which exists side by side with it, it possesses a vegetation which has all the appearance of having existed at that spot from of old. So unlike the barren, thistly, and weedy waste lands and fallows does it look, so harmonious, so natural all that grows upon it, that in some cases you would find it hard to believe that the plant life is not native, but has migrated hither, and was only able to take permanent hold of the soil because of the destruction of the turf. These plants came in fact as weeds, but have long established their position as members of the flora of the downs, albeit in their larger growth, social habits, and shorter life they differ markedly from the older flora of the turf.

The most curious thing about this vegetation of the lands that have been tilled very many years ago is that it varies in an extraordinary degree in different places. A slight difference in the local conditions, as, for instance, depth of soil, etc., in different hills, or different spots on the same hill, has probably brought about this result. At one place two or three species have by chance fallen upon a suitable unoccupied spot, after the turf has been killed, and have spread over it and continued in possession ever since; but on the next spot different species have colonised. Some of these places are overgrown with tall grass, a monotonous green, with scarcely a flower among it; but in most places the eye is caught by colour, and the colour will be yellow, red, blue, purple, or white, according to the species that predominate; or it may be blue and yellow, or red and white, or a mixture of all colours.

Another marked difference between the true native flora of the turf, and these intruders which have become natives, is in the longer life, or at all events more lasting freshness, of the former. Except in very dry seasons, when the intense heat burns the hills brown, the turf is always green and blossoming from March to October. The colonising grasses and herbs are at their best in May and June.

A noteworthy fact about these wild chance-made gardens scattered far and wide over the downs is that, besides their variety and beauty, there is in some a singularity which adds to their attractiveness, and causes them to be vividly remembered afterwards. This is not solely caused by the contrast of patches or islands of vegetation unlike that about it, which gives it something of an exotic appearance, but also by colour effects not often seen. Some of the prettiest effects are found on spots where it may be said that "nothing grows"—nothing, that is to say, from the agriculturist's and the shepherd's points of view, where there is an exceedingly thin soil on summits and high slopes, and the plough having once broken up and ruined the ancient turf has made the ground barren for ever. Two such spots I will describe.

On one the thin poor soil was of a fine red colour, thinly overgrown with an extraordinary variety of plants, with fine wiry stems and few and scanty leaves, but with flowers almost normal as to size. There was nowhere a mass or patch of bright colour, but over the whole surface a sprinkling of yellow, red, white, purple, and blue colour, the flowers everywhere mixed with golden brown and silvery brown grasses, while under this thin herbage appeared the red ground flecked with white flints. It was a curiously beautiful and fascinating picture. There is nothing in art that can give us any idea of effects of this kind, which are not uncommon in nature; but I suppose it is a fact that artists do sometimes attempt to produce them; and if we have never seen the originals, or having seen can blot them out, their attempts may not seem wholly futile. We may see it, for instance, in some exceedingly beautiful examples of the potter's art, when every colour used in painting clay has been thrown upon a vase or plaque and by chance a happy effect has resulted. We see it too in some old Persian and Turkish carpets, in which a variety of very pure and beautiful colours are woven in a fabric without design or pattern. Again, we get an effect of this kind in a few stained-glass windows.

The one I have in my mind at this moment has given me more pleasure than any other window in any church or cathedral in England; and it is without design, for it was destroyed some three or four centuries ago, but the fragments were gathered up by pious hands, and after many years restored to their place pieced anyhow together.

A second even more barren spot, a couple of miles from the one described, was, so far as my experience goes, absolutely unique in character, and as simple and chaste in its one beautiful colour as the other was rich and varied with its sprinkling of half a hundred colours. Walking on the long plateau-like top of the high down I saw before me a perfectly white piece of ground, an area of about twelve to fourteen acres, and concluded that it was an old ploughed field overgrown with white campion; but on arriving at the place I found that my sheet of white blossoms was nothing but a field thickly strewn with white flints. It is often said, and it is perhaps true, that the flints of the chalk downs after exposure to the air become whiter than any other flints; and these were white indeed—white as white blossoms in summer, and as a field covered with snow in winter. That any spot with so thin a soil, where the blanket or matting of the turf must have rested on a bed of flinty chalk, had been thought worth cultivating was something to wonder at. Now, until I was within twenty or thirty yards of this stony field, where it touched the green turf, it appeared absolutely without any plant life, but at that short distance I found that it was overgrown with forget-me-not, a plant that, like the pimpernel, is always found on waste stony or barren places on the downs where the turf has been destroyed. But in most places it grows among other plants: here it had the whole field to itself, and grew to a height of nine or ten inches; its exceedingly thin, dark-coloured, wire-like, leafless stems crowned with their loose clusters of minute turquoise blue blossoms. The smallness of the flowers and thread-like fineness of the stems had made them invisible until seen close at hand, and then how beautiful they looked! The whole level expanse, thick strewn with shining white flints, appeared covered with a thin veil or mist of a most exquisite blue.

Of the more splendid—one might almost say bizarre—effects, caused by masses of bright-coloured flowers, a good many instances could be given if space allowed. One must suffice. This was a very dense growth of viper's bugloss covering about an acre of ground on the summit of a down east of the Cuckmere stream. This plant usually grows scattered about even when most abundant, as I have found it in some spots in Suffolk: here the rough stalks studded with their intense blue flowers grew thick as corn, one other plant with them—namely, the large woolly thistle, which grew to the same height as the bugloss stalks, and had flowers of an enormous size. One of these big flower-heads would have filled a small coffee-cup. It struck me as most curious that the purple of the thistle and the bright blue of the bugloss looked so well together; but the sight was a very beautiful as well as a singular one.

I will here remark that large masses of blue flowers seen under a blue sky in a strong light, however novel and enchanting the sight may be as long as the vision rests on it, does not leave as distinct and vivid a picture on the mind as masses of flowers of any other colour seen in similar conditions. It is true that a sheet of wild hyacinths in a wood in spring is a beautiful sight that we never forget. But in this case there is a background of trees, and deep shadow and green above, between the blue of the flowers and the blue of the sky.

My mention of the big or woolly thistle reminds me of another pretty effect of a colonising flower on the downs which I should not perhaps have thought much about but for an incident and an attractive human figure in the picture.

During a walk among the South Downs one day in June, looking up from the valley I was in, I saw far up near the top of the hill in front of me a shepherd boy standing motionless, his crook in his hand, his dog, held by a cord or chain, at his side. Wishing to have a talk with him I began the ascent of the rather steep slope, and he, divining my intention, waited for me. As I came close to him he made a very pretty picture, standing against the blue sky knee-deep in the tall grass, just beginning to flower, which covered that part of the down. Among the grass sainfoin grew abundantly, and the green grass was sprinkled everywhere with the rose-red of its blossoming spikes. Even a very few flowers of any other colour would have taken something from the exquisite beauty of that chance green and rose-red arrangement. But there were no other flowers. The young shepherd, aged about fifteen, had one of those perfectly Saxon faces which you see more in Sussex than anywhere in England—a large round face, rosy brown in colour, shy blue eyes and light brown hair, worn long. The expression, the shy yet pleased look —pleased that the monotony of his long solitary day would be broken by this chance encounter with a stranger—was childlike and very pretty. He had loose-fitting grey clothes on, and a round grey peak-less cap; and for ornament he had fastened in the middle of it, where there had perhaps once been a top-knot or ball, a big woolly thistle flower. It was really very curious to note how that one big thorny flower-head with its purple disc harmonised with everything about the boy and gave him a strange distinction.

Most of the colonising plants on the downs have, as I have said, their period of greatest beauty in May and June: the common field scabious is an exception. Like the blue devil's-bit scabious it is also found on the turf; but it flourishes chiefly on (and on account of its long stem is best suited to) the grass lands that have once been tilled. In such localities it is very common and outlasts all its neighbours of other species, and a very pretty effect is sometimes produced by that flower "blooming alone" when abundant in the tall grass burnt yellow by the heats of July and August. The pale mauve-blue of the flower and pale yellow of the grass are complementary colours, and almost as pleasing as the rose-red of sainfoin blossom with the vivid green of June grass.

When these wild gardens of the old broken-up grounds are sere and flowerless, or the flowers are few, the downs where the turf has never been destroyed still glow with colour as in spring; and it is then most delightful to visit those wilder places where many hours, or even a whole day, may be spent out of sight of any human form, not even excepting a solitary shepherd, standing motionless and statuesque on the side of a distant hill.

Happily such desert spots still exist, wild as when the vanished bustard had his home in them; miles upon miles of rough vegetation; acres of luxuriant furze, flowerless now at the end of summer, darkest green with a bloom of lighter green, bluish in tint, on its tops. The furze is like the pine in this; and looking down upon it one can fancy oneself a Titan standing waist-deep in a vast pine-forest, with the blue-green feathery tree-tops all about one. Elsewhere the furze may be seen growing among other bushes, appearing as blotches of darkest green among greens of various lighter shades; trailing brambles, and briars still waving aloft a few white and red roses; and in and out among them, hanging everywhere in beautiful rags, and binding bush to bush with ropes of many-shaped leaves, convolvulus and fragrant woodbine, wild clematis in its silky beard, and bryony beaded with green and scarlet berries. Among the bushes on the lower slopes one stumbles on places of extraordinary fertility, where the thistle, foxglove, ragwort, viper's bugloss, agrimony, and wild mignonette grow to a man's breast; while over them all the mullein lifts its great flowery rod to a height of six to nine feet. From these luxuriant patches you pass to more open ground covered with golden seeding grasses, and heather, fiery purple-red, and emerald-green spots powdered white with woodruff, and patches of purple thyme. One afternoon, tired with a long day's ramble in the burning sun, I cast myself down on one of these fragrant beds and fell into a doze. That night when I threw off my clothes I noticed that the fragrance still clung to them, and when I woke next morning the air of the room was so charged with it that for a moment I fancied myself still out of doors, where I had fallen asleep on that purple flowery bed.

The heather on the downs is of two species—the pale purple ling, or dwarf heath, and the fiery purple-red small-leafed heath. I decline to call it by its common but absurd name—absurd, I mean, when speaking of it as a common plant of the Sussex Downs. From July to September is the blossoming time of the heath, but at one favoured spot I have found the small-leafed species in fullest bloom in June; and as in this instance heather and June-flowering dropwort were blossoming together, where there was no other plant to spoil the harmony, a unique and very striking effect was produced. The dropwort is found all over the chalk hills, everywhere a smaller, neater plant than its great, tall, rank cousin of the moist meads, the fragrant meadowsweet. On the close-cropped turf of the downs the dropwort may be seen flowering with no more than a couple of inches of stem, but when it grows among furze or heather it sends up a stem from a foot to eighteen inches high. At the spot I have spoken of, the fiery blossoms of the heather covered an area of about three-quarters of an acre, on the slope of a furzy down, and over the whole of the ground the dropwort grew, sprinkled so evenly and abundantly that almost every square yard of ground had its one slim stem crowned with its loose cream-coloured cluster. Not a leaf does this plant show—nothing but the slim tall stem with its flower-cluster rising several inches above the level of the rough heather; the intense purple-red glow of the myriads of small heath bells, massed, or thickly sprinkled over the dusky green of the ground; above, the slender stems waving their small creamy-white flags and rags of blossoms in the wind; —the effect of the whole, the contrast in form and colour, the airy motions of one and immobility of the other, was most fascinating.

One of the latest summer flowers of the downs, which is so abundant as to give a colour to the scene in some spots, is the harebell. It is a dainty flower, airy and delicate in shape, waving or trembling to every breath on its hair-like stem, of an exquisite tender blue, the nearest, I think, of any flower to the cerulean hue of the small butterfly's wings. It blooms everywhere on the hills from July to September, but is most abundant about the end of August; and one cannot help wondering to see this frail flower looking its brightest and best—"enjoying the air it breathes"—when the weather is dryest and hottest. Like the dropwort, it abounds more and grows tallest when it has the protection of some thorny or uneatable plant—heath, furze, or bitter grass. On some of the high downs a grass grows which the sheep refuse to touch; it is dull green in colour, changing to greenish-brown in late summer, and grows thickly and evenly over the ground to a height of five or six inches, forming a soft carpet which is pleasant to walk on. The shepherds call it "ur-grass. " I am not sure about the spelling, but it is pronounced something like "ugh! "—a familiar grunt of exclamation of disgust. The summit of Ditchling Beacon, the highest point of the South Downs (and of Sussex), is clothed with this grass, and at the end of last August, after the long excessively hot season, before any rain had fallen, the harebells were so abundant as to give a blue tinge to the earth. While resting on the ground at this spot, it occurred to me to measure a square yard of the surface and count the fully-open blossoms contained within that space. They numbered sixty-four. Before finishing with this part of the subject it may be observed that on these high, treeless downs, in the burning sun, the flowers are more intense in colour than those that bloom in the shade and close shelter of the woods and forests of the weald, even those of the same species—the poor

Half-faded blossoms, pale with heat
And full of bitter summer.

Looking round upon the living garment of many colours, especially where the glowing orange-yellow patches of ragwort are most conspicuous, one can fancy that the strayed pack-horses of a silk merchant of the olden time have passed this way, and that the sharp claws of the bramble have caught and pulled the packages to pieces, scattering far and wide the shining fabrics of all the hues in the rainbow. This brilliancy in the colour of the flowers has a counterpart in the greater intensity of life in the creatures; or so it seems to me. The hum of the bees; the lightning-quick movement of the lizard and of the adder, when one is so fortunate as to catch a glimpse of him—a sinuous, swift-moving band of a shining golden-brown colour; the frantic scuttling into cover of the disturbed rabbit; the lively movements and music of the small birds—all give one the idea that the hottest time of the summer is their period of greatest activity.

These blossoming places in the wilderness which I have tried to describe, and which make the thought of our trim, pretty artificial gardens a weariness, are not too many: in most places the untilled downs are bare of furze and bramble and the plants that take advantage of the bramble's protection, and are close-cropped by the sheep. Their very smoothness gives them a character which is quite unique and has a peculiar charm. Flowers are abundant and in considerable variety, but many that are luxuriant in rich soils, wherever there is shelter and protection, here scarcely look like the same species: they have changed their habits of growth, their form and size, to suit the different conditions. The luxury of long stems, the delight of waving in the wind, and the ambition to overtop their neighbours, would here be fatal. Their safety lies in nestling down amid the lowly grass, keeping so close to the earth as to be able to blossom and ripen their seed in spite of the ever-nibbling sheep—the living lawn-mowers perpetually moving about over them. The vegetation has the appearance of a beautiful tapestry worked in various shades of green, roughened with the slender dry bents standing out like pale yellow thread-ends from the green texture; flecked, and in places splashed with brilliant colour—red, purple, blue, and yellow. Or if you look at the flowers with the sun before you they appear like shining gems sewn into the fabric and forming an irregular pattern. The commonest flowers of the close-fed downs are mostly quite small. Commonest in spring, when indeed yellow flowers most abound, is the bird-foot trefoil. The wee fairy yellow trefoil is common, too; and clovers red and clovers white; and the kidney vetch, with curious embossed or jewelled flower-heads. Creeping rock-rose with soft, silky petals, and clustered bell-flower, deep blue, looking like Canterbury bells picked from their stalk and scattered about on the grass. Crane's-bill and musky stork's-bill—mere specks of red; little round-leaved mint, a faint misty purple; and the scented plantain, its leaves like leaves cut out of green cloth, pressed flat and sewn upon the green fabric. Rest-harrow, very dark green on a light green turf, with minute pink and white butterfly blossoms. Woodruff, round and among the furze bushes, like powdery snow newly fallen on the green earth: and curiously named squinancy-wort, exceeding small and fragrant, blooming all over the turfy downs, here white, there rose-red, or deep red, or purple, so variable is it in colour. More abundant still, and more variable, is the minute milkwort, quaintly and prettily described by old Gerarde: "The flower grows at the top of a blew colour, fashioned like a little bird, with wings, tail, and body, only to be discovered by those who do observe the same. " It is indeed blue in many places, as if a summer shower of blue rain had fallen from an unclouded sky, and the small stems were still beaded with the drops; but by-and-by, as you walk over the downs, you will find—if you do observe the same—that the flower is getting a paler and paler blue, and finally your little milkwort is seen to be purest white. Continuing your walk again, you will soon be in some place where the tiny bird-blossom will have a rosy blush, and to the blushing flowers will succeed pink, then red, then purple, and then blue again. It is interesting to note that the different colours are not often seen together, or in one place. Blue, white, pink, and purple flowers are all at some distance apart, although all may be found on one hill, with flowers of intermediate shades between. Thus we see that in this species the colour is not fixed and the mark of a distinct variety, as in the pimpernel and other species which produce flowers of different colours. The colour of the milkwort probably depends on the character of the soil, or some other local condition. Has anyone ever tried the experiment of growing the plant in beds from seeds produced by flowers of different colours? Observant old Gerarde described them all separately, and made their number six. "The fourth kind, " he says, "is like the last in every respect, but that it hath white floures, otherwise it is very like. " Then he says: "The purple milkwort differeth from the others in the colour of its floures, wherein especially consisteth the difference. " And finally, his sixth milkwort "is like unto the rest in each respect, saving that the floures are of an overworn ill-favoured colour, which maketh it to differ from the others of its kind. "

Next to the delight of flowers themselves is to me that of listening to the old herbalist discoursing of the same; and this would I say of no other work on plant-lore, for these are mostly a weariness to read. The old author is simple, not concerning himself overmuch about the reason of things, or, as he would say, he loveth not to dance in quagmires. And sometimes he is almost childlike in his repetitions and reaffirmations; but the colour of his style is never overworn, and he is for ever fresh and full of variety and agreeable surprises, like Nature herself, who maketh her plants not for meat and medicine only, but some to be esteemed for beauty alone, and as garlands and crowns for pleasure. Indeed, there is not seldom a lustre in his words that serves to remind one of the red whortle he greatly admired, which is full of juice of so orient and beautiful a colour to limn withal that Indian lacca cannot be compared thereunto. Nor let it be forgot that it was he who invented the name of Traveller's Joy; and by increasing the pleasure which all have in that green and silver adorner of our country waysides and hedges, may even be said to have added something to nature.

It would not be possible to mention all nor half the numerous small pretty flowering herbs that mingle their roots in the close matting of the turf that covers the sheep-fed downs; but a word must be said of the eyebright, that minute shrub a couple of inches high, deepest green in colour, with many small yet conspicuous blossoms, white and rose-colour, streaked with purple, and for the pupil of its eye, one spot of divine yellow. It is a flower that brightens the eye that sees it, since no person can look at it and not feel gladdened at the sight. It blossoms from July to October, and I always find it on very steep slippery downs, often where the chalk crops out of the thin soil, and I imagine the cause of this to be that this plant to save itself must be out of reach of the nibbling sheep. All other herbs may be eaten down often to the roots without being destroyed or defeated in their object of ripening their seed at last; but at the slightest pull the eyebright comes up, root and branch, and I think that most if not all of the plants that grow on accessible ground must get eaten up before they can ripen their seed. Why the plant comes up so easily in the sheep's mouth, or in your hand if you attempt ever so gently to pull one small flowering branchlet, is the eyebright's secret. The plant is supposed to be a semi-parasite that feeds on the roots of other plants, and on examining a piece of turf you find that its root-stems scarcely penetrate to the soil under the mat of roots of the other plants; that from its root-stems very fine hair-like fibres branch out, and are loosely fastened to the grass roots; but whether these fine fibres suck the sap of the roots they attach themselves to, or merely feed on exudations and other neglected or rejected materials, the botanists are not yet able to tell us.

Among the numerous small blooms of the downs, a few of which I have named, there is one that is big, comparatively—the largest, most conspicuous, and most generally distributed all over the chalk hills. This is the dwarf or plume thistle. Its leaves you do not notice, nor even see unless you look for them, for, like the plantain leaves, they are found close to the ground; sewn, so to speak, into the fabric of the turf. The solitary flower-head is practically stemless, and rests like a cup or vase on the earth—a great amethyst among gems of other colours and of smaller size.

Though it looks so big among the little blooms, you see that it is not really big when the queen humble-bee drops upon it and well-nigh blots out its purple disc with her large, black, hairy body.

CHAPTER IV

A FAIRY FAUNA

Insect life of the downs—Common snail—Adder-like colouring of some snails—The "thrushes' anvil"—Eccentric motions of flies—Peculiar colouring of some flies—The cow-dung fly—A thyme-loving fly—Butterflies—Disposition and habits of the small blue—Sleep in insects—The humble-bee—Intoxicating effect of thistle flower on bees—The unknown faculties of insects—De Quincey's "gluttonism. "

In the last chapter we had an account of a fairy flora, as we call the numerous minute herbaceous plants, mixed with small grasses and clovers, which clothe the sheep-fed downs in a grassy and flowery mantle. The fairy flora has a fairy fauna to match it. Where there is no bush vegetation nor heath and rough herbage for shelter, there are no birds. At all events none breed on the naked unsheltered ground, unless it be a wheatear that makes his nest in an old rabbit-hole in some open stony spot. But of the birds and beasts of downland I shall treat in the next chapter. The creatures that mostly impress us in all the open shelterless places are the insects. We think less of the innumerable small inconspicuous snails, whitey-grey like the small fragments of chalk seen in the turf; indeed we think of them not at all unless we hear by chance the crunching of their frail shells beneath our soles as we walk. Alas, that, glad to exist ourselves, we should thus unwittingly tread out so many small sparks of life!

A word here about our common banded snail (*Helix nemoralis*), which is common everywhere in the furzy places, but is incapable of existence on the close-cropped turf. Everyone knows how extremely variable in colour the shell of this snail is; in every garden a pretty collection may be made of shells, red, yellow, cream, and brown of many shades; shells marked and unmarked, with great variety, too, in their markings. Now most of the shells I see on the downs are of one type; indeed, you may in some parts search the furzy spots for miles without getting a snail of any other type. The ground colour is yellow, or yellowish white, with broad black longitudinal bands. Not only is it a most conspicuous coloration, but seen casually down among the vivid green of the furze and herbage it often startles a person by its curiously close resemblance to a small portion of a highly-coloured adder's coil. This chance resemblance to a dangerous creature does not, however, serve the snail as a protection from his principal enemies, the thrushes. Wherever there is a patch of furze there you will find the "thrushes' anvil, " usually a flint half or nearly quite buried in the soil a few feet away from the bushes, and all round the anvil the turf is strewn with shattered shells.

To return to the insects of the downs. Of these flies thrust themselves most on our attention; it is, in fact, impossible to overlook creatures that conduct themselves in so wildly eccentric a manner. One big yellow fly like a honey-bee comes directly at you with a loud hostile hum or buzz, hovers for a few moments, dashes away in a straight line, turns off at a tangent, and, rushing back again, proceeds with extraordinary velocity to describe curves and circles, parallel lines, angles, and other geometric figures in the air; and finally drops down within a few inches of you, to remain motionless as a fly carved out of a yellow pebble until the impulse sends him off again. What his motives are, what it all means, we are unable to guess; we can only conclude in our ignorance, judging from appearances, that he is mad; that, in fact, the proverbial March hare is a preeminently sane and sensible creature in comparison. Somewhat of this light-headedness is, I imagine, seen in most of the flies, from the burliest bluebottle to the small gilded variety. What would it be, I wonder, if these minute creatures grew to the size of ducks and geese? Our whole time would be spent in watching their amazing, meaningless antics; nothing else would be talked or even thought about in the world. In the end, we should become strictly nocturnal, in order to be out of their way, or else we should ourselves go mad in their company.

The peculiarity of another species, which is like a house-fly in size and shape, is in his colouring; on his jet-black body he wears a broad transverse crimson bar. Of this pretty, most singular fly there is a pleasant story to tell. In August, when he abounds most, wild thyme is in the height of its blossoming season in many places on the downs, both in the hills and in the deep vales and hollows; and its round patches of deep green creeping plants, purpled over with bloom, are exceedingly conspicuous on the paler green or yellow or grey-brown of the turf. To these small islands of fragrance the fly resorts, and the whole island or patch may sometimes be found swarming with them.

Does the unentomological reader happen to know an insect, a fly, of quaint and curious aspect, known to many persons by the good, honest, vernacular name of cow-dung fly, and regarded by some good people as an ugly, repulsive-looking, hump-backed, hairy creature? It is an Asilus—a big fly that slays and devours other flies, even as we kill and eat cows, sheep, and many other creatures more innocent and beautiful than ourselves. In spring this fly spreads all over the country, especially in meadows and grass lands, where he exhibits that extraordinary predilection for cow-dung which gives him his name. To a piece of fresh cow-dung they flock in such numbers that it is soon covered with a dense mass of them, their yellow, hairy, round-backed bodies making it look like an embossed mound of dark gold. The exact hue closely resembles what we call "old gold, " or gold without the glint. When disturbed they rise up with a loud buzz like a swarm of angry wasps, and after wheeling about in a confused noisy cloud for a few moments they settle again, and the mound of old gold is formed once more. It is a fascinating sight; and a nature-lover of a sensibility as exquisite as that of Charles Lamb, when he looked at the Fleet Street crowd at eleven o'clock at night, might, too, shed "tears of happiness at the sight of so much life. "

Now, just as the cow-dung attracts the great golden fly, so does the purple patch of thyme attract the smaller crimson-banded fly of the downs. I suppose it is the scent that draws him, and possibly they go to it more for pleasure than profit; at all events, they are not so much occupied in feeding on the flowers as in rapidly moving about over and among them; not flying but creeping and running hither and thither, crossing and recrossing each other's track in every direction, a maze of black and red flies performing a sort of complicated dance, all agitating and waving their glistening wings, as if that bath of sweetness had made them mad with delight.

Some of my readers may be inclined to ask—Why, when describing an interesting habit of any creature, do I not give the scientific name? Well, it would undoubtedly be easy to do so in some cases; for instance, when speaking of the common or house sparrow, or the stag-beetle, it would be easy to follow the example of those writers who besprinkle their pages with the learned names of every familiar creature. But the flies are a small and an exceedingly numerous people. When you happen on a fly that by chance draws your attention by its curious actions or appearance, it is not so easy as the uninformed person may think to give it a name; I have tried it and therefore know. I have consulted books and books, and found not what I sought: I have also consulted entomologists, and they have asked me in a tone of surprise and mild remonstrance if I had taken them for Dipterists, when, as I ought to have known, they were Lepidopterists, or else Coleopterists. This is indeed the poor, puzzled field naturalist's great trouble, that so many monograph compilers occupy themselves with these two great orders of insects, while other orders, just as interesting when you come to look at the creatures, are neglected. Well, it is a comfort to hear that there *is* a Dipterist in England, and that he has nearly finished writing the very book that many of us want—a monograph of the British flies.

Butterflies are abundant; a brimstone yellow shining in the sunlight has a very splendid appearance as he flutters airily by you on his way; but the larger brilliant-coloured species rest not here, where the green flowery surface is too smooth for them. The red admiral is common enough in furzy places; but on the close-cropped turf the largest butterfly is the grey heath—the sedentary "gatekeeper, " who seldom flies until disturbed. A brown, a skipper, the small heath, a small copper—these are some of the most common species. Most abundant is the little pale blue of the chalk downs; in fact, he outnumbers all the others together. Sitting on the grass, you can sometimes count as many as thirty or forty fluttering about in sight and near you at one time. It is curious to note that the hue of the sky and atmosphere on this insect's wings appears to have "entered his soul, " to make him more aerial in habits, more light-hearted and playful in disposition than his other-coloured relations. If one has ever seen the great blue Morpho butterfly of the tropics, one recalls its wonderful beauty, soaring high in the sunlight, its colour changing in depth at every moment; now pale as our pale little blue of the downs, now azure, now deepest sapphire; and now flashing white as polished silver, or as crystal. This is the angel among butterflies, as our small blue of the downs is the fairy; and, wide apart as they are, it is the heavenly hue in both that distinguishes them above other creatures of their class.

As a compensation for their greater activity the little blues have a shorter day than the other kinds; like little children who have been running about playing all day long, they go to bed early. Before six o'clock, when other butterflies are still abroad and active, when the sun is more than two hours from setting, and the humble-bee has yet two hours of labour before him, they are tired out and their briefer day is finished. Now most butterflies when they go to rest tumble anyhow into bed; in other words, they creep or drop into the herbage, take hold of a stem, and go to sleep in any position, their appearance being that of a dead or faded leaf. The blue has a quite different habit. As a rule, even where the down is smoothest and without shelter, there exist slight hollows or depressions, where the grass is higher and rougher than in other places; and to such spots the blues gather from all around; but instead of creeping down into the grass, they settle on the very tips of the dry bents. At some spots in an area of a few square yards they may be found in scores; one or two or three, and sometimes as many as half a dozen, on one bent, sitting head down, the closed wings appearing like a sharp-pointed grey leaflet at the end of the stem. It is hard to believe that they can really be asleep, sitting thus exposed, their great black eyes looking very wide awake, the afternoon sun pouring its light into their tiny brains; but when touched they scarcely move, and they will even suffer you to pick them off and replace them on the bent without flying away; and there they will remain through the night, however strong the wind may blow.

What we call sleep in an insect resembles the somnambulistic state, rather then sleep as we experience it. Thus this resting butterfly can be made to act, and he usually does the right thing. He keeps his hold on the bent when the wind beats, and when after being plucked off he is replaced, he grasps it firmly again; finally, when tossed up, he flies away and slants down until he touches the grass, then fastens himself once more to a stem; but there is no doubt that he does it all unconsciously, like a person in a hypnotic condition doing what he has been willed to do.

The little blue butterfly's habit of roosting on the tips of the bents is, I imagine, advantageous, and may be one cause of the abundance of this species. At sunset, if you narrowly observe the ground in one of those depressions or hollows where the grass grows thickest and tallest, and which are the sleeping-places of all the small butterflies and other diurnal insects of the downs, you will be surprised at the number of the rapacious species of various kinds to be seen busily quartering the ground like so many wood-ants in quest of prey. They do not climb to the tops of the smooth slender bents, and the small blue is therefore safe from them; but it is a wonder that any of the skippers and other species that creep into the shelter of the grass should escape the multitude of insect foxes, cats, and weasels prowling about in search of a meal.

When all the small butterflies and diurnal flies and beetles and the quaint goat-faced grasshopper have gone to rest, the humble-bee is still at work. No short day for him! (*It* or *her* it ought to be, but let that pass.) He reminds me of a London omnibus-driver who was talked to by a zealous Socialistic friend of mine on the advantages of an eight-hours' day. His reply was, "I don't at all hold with them principles. Ain't a day got twenty-four hours? And what does that mean? It means, I take it, that there's twelve hours for work and twelve for rest. Half one and half the other. There's no getting over that—it's too plain. I've always worked twelve hours a day, and, say what you like, I ain't going against nature. "

That is also the humble-bee's philosophy; but although he is very stable-minded there are moments when he is tempted to depart from it. The thistle flower overcomes him with its deliciousness, and he will stick to it, feasting on its sweets, forgetful of the community's claim on him and of the law of his being, until he is no longer in a fit condition to go home. At all events, he refuses to do so. Walking about on the downs in the fading light you will find the belated reveller half buried in the purple disc, clasping it affectionately to his bosom; and however stupefied with nectar he may seem, you will observe that he still continues to thrust at the small tubular florets with his proboscis, although probably with a very uncertain aim. If you compassionately touch him with a finger-tip to remind him of the lateness of the hour, he will lurch over to one side and put out one or two of his anterior legs or arms to make a gesture waving you off. And if your ears were tuned to catch the small inaudible sounds of nature, you would doubtless hear him exclaiming with indistinct utterance, "Go 'way; for goo'ness sake don't'sturb me; lemme be— I'm a' right. "

It is noticeable that even in his cups he never wholly loses the characteristic dignity of manner coupled with gentleness we so greatly admire in him. There may be in his order creatures equally intelligent, but morally, or at all events in manner, he is decidedly their superior. So peaceable and mild in disposition is he, so regardful of the rights of others, even of the meanest, that he will actually give place to a fly coming to feed at the same flower. It is on this account that, alone among insects, the humble-bee is universally regarded with esteem and affection. In his virtues, and in all that is best in him, he is very human. It is therefore not strange, during a late walk, when we bid good-night and goodbye to the darkening downs, that it grieves us a little to find so estimable an insect in such a plight.

We often say, and it is easily said, that this or that animal is human-like; but if the truth could be known about such matters we should probably find that the social humble-bee, with all his virtues, is just as far removed from us as any other creature with an articulated cylindrical body. It is sad to think, or so it appears to me after a day agreeably spent on the downs in the society of this small people, that in spite of all our prying into nature's secrets, all our progress and the vast accumulations of knowledge at our disposal, we do not and never can know what an insect knows or feel what it feels. What appearance this visible world has to an eye with twenty thousand facets to it is beyond our power to imagine or conceive. Nay, more, we know that these small bodies have windows and avenues which ours are without; that they are conscious of vibrations which for us do not exist; that millions of "nimble emanations, " which miss us in spite of our large size, hit them. We can gaze through a magnifying-glass at certain of their complex organs of sense, but cannot conjecture their use. They are as great a mystery or as meaningless to us as our most delicate and complicated scientific instruments would seem to a wild man of the woods. If it were not for our limitations—if we could go a little beyond our tether—we could find out the cause of the seemingly mad behaviour of the fly.

De Quincey wrote very prettily about what he called "gluttonism"—the craving of the mind to know and enjoy all the good literature and music and art-work that had been produced; and finally to know the lives of all men—all who are living and all who had lived on the earth. It strikes one that this craving, as he described it, though he says that it afflicts us all, and that he himself had been reduced to an extremity of wretchedness by it, must be set down as one of the many inventions of that fascinating but insincere writer. Speaking for myself, if the power to attain to all that De Quincey craved, or pretended that he craved for, were mine, I should not value it; I should give it all to be able to transform myself for the space of a summer's day into one of these little creatures on the South Downs; then to return to my own form and place in nature with a clear recollection of the wonderland in which I had been. And if, in the first place, I were permitted to select my own insect, I should carefully consider them all, since they differ as greatly from each other as bird from serpent, and fish from mammal. I should pass in review the slow beetle, heavily armoured, and the fantastic fly, a miracle of inconsequence; the esteemed humble-bee, and the wasp, that very fine insect gentleman in his mood of devilish cheerfulness; the diligent ant, absorbed in his minute business; the grasshopper, with his small stringed instrument and long grave countenance; and the dragon-fly, with those two great gem-like orbs that reflect a nature of an unimaginable aspect. And after all I should make choice of the little blue butterfly, despite his smallness and frivolity, to house myself in.

The knowledge of that strange fairy world it inhabits would be incommunicable, like the vision vouchsafed to some religionist of which he has been forbidden to speak; but the memory of it would be a secret perennial joy.

CHAPTER V

WILD LIFE

Wild life confined to the furze—The rabbit and his enemy—
The fox abundant—A badgers' earth—Tenacity of the
badger—Dead shrews—Moles without water—Catching
moles for fun—A shepherd on moles—Birds—Extinct
species—A shepherd's reminiscences—Buzzards building
on bushes—Black game in Ashdown Forest—The last stone
curlew—Long-eared owl—Pre-natal suggestion in the lower
animals—Existing large birds—A colony of gulls at
Seaford—Kestrel preying on grasshoppers—Turtle-dove—
Missel-thrush and small birds—Wheatears and sea-
poppies—Shrike—The common lizard's weakness—Sheep
killed by adders—Beauty of the adder—A handful of
adders—Shepherd boy and big snake.

The very small animal life, the fairy fauna as I have called it, is that
of the close-cropped turf; the larger wild life of bird and beast and
reptile is almost exclusively confined to the rough spots overgrown
with furze, bramble, and other bush and dwarf-tree vegetation, in
some places intermixed with bracken and heather. These rough
isolated places are sometimes like islands on a wide expanse of
smooth turf; and for those who love wildness, and wild creatures,
they are often delightful spots in which to spend a long summer's
day. Here the creatures live a comparatively undisturbed life; at all
events it may be said that they are not much disturbed by man out of
the shooting and hunting seasons. There are partridges, mostly red-
legs, and a few wild pheasants in some places, and rabbits
everywhere. Seeing these last so abundant and so tame in the
presence of man, one might imagine that an island of furze on the
downs is a perfect paradise for bunny all the summer long; but it is
not so; his chiefest and most subtle enemy, the fox, is always lurking
near, watching him in all his outgoings and incomings. I doubt that
foxes are anywhere in England more numerous than in some of the
furze-grown places on the South Downs. It is true they are hunted in
their season, else they would not be in existence at all, but I do not
think that more than one fox in every six or eight born each year is
killed by the hounds. How they are kept within reasonable limits I
cannot say; I can only say that some of them do meet with a violent
death, during the summer months, in spite of the strong feeling in

favour of their preservation among the farmers. As a rule the farmer declines to make any claim for lambs destroyed, and if his wife sends in a claim for a dozen or twenty chickens taken, she gets a sympathetic message, possibly a pair of gloves, from the M. F.H., and there the matter ends. Still, the red rascal does often meet with his deserts; I have found foxes at midsummer, in fine condition and with a splendid coat of hair, lying dead among the furze, and could only say, "Careless fellow! you have gone and got yourself bitten by an adder, and there's an end of you. "

In spite of hounds and "adders, " the fox continues only too numerous. In the course of one morning's walk I have come upon four foxes in a furzy down, and where I saw four there must have been forty.

The badger, too, still exists in some of the rough furzy spots. At one place in the South Downs I discovered an earth in the centre of a large clump of old furze, mixed with elder bushes, growing on an exceedingly steep slope, where a man could hardly stand upright. In the middle of the clump there were five great holes and an enormous heap of flints and lumps of hard chalk, many of them weighing six to seven pounds. These badgers must indeed have possessed an amazing strength to make their earth in such a place. The trunks and low horizontal branches of the elder bushes had been used, some to rub their hide on and some to clean their clay-covered feet, so that some were rubbed smooth and others plastered with clay. The floors of the burrows as far down as one could see and feel were thickly carpeted with freshly-gathered moss, carried down to form the nest.

It struck me very forcibly when viewing this earth, and thinking of its occupant's tremendous power, tenacity, and hardiness, and of his excessive shyness and strictly nocturnal habits, that, in spite of his rarity, he may yet win in the race of life with his more numerous and protected neighbour, the fox. That fox-hunting will eventually die out as a national sport in this country is now a common belief even among those who pursue it with the greatest enthusiasm; and when that time arrives there will be nothing to save the fox from the fate of the wolf, the marten, and the wild cat; unless indeed a new sentiment should spring up in the place of the existing one to preserve him as a member of the British fauna—a sentiment similar to that which has preserved the useless heron in this country, and is now saving the golden eagle from extermination in the north of Scotland. It is so easy to kill the fox, and he is such a destructive beast, that half a century hence we can imagine the farmer and henwife saying, "If the fox is wanted alive for the sake of his beauty, or for some such reason, the good people who want him must pay for his keep, otherwise it must be a life for a life. "

But the badger is not destructive; or at all events the damage he inflicts on the farmer is comparatively insignificant, and he is very hard to kill. Though our largest savage beast he has, up till now, maintained his existence throughout the length and breadth of the land, in spite of much persecution; and we now see that there is growing up a feeling in favour of his preservation, which will make his position safer.

I learned on inquiry that the badgers whose earth I had found were not in any danger of being disturbed, and I was told of a second earth a few miles from the first where the animals were also allowed to be at peace.

The stoat is not uncommon on the downs, and loyally aids the fox in his labour of keeping the rabbits down. The common shrew also abounds, although these high and excessively dry hills strike one as a most unsuitable district for such an animal. And here as in other places it is a common thing to find these quaint little creatures lying dead in bare open spots. All the dead shrews I have examined on the downs had been killed, and from the crushed condition of some of them I take it that the fox, like the cat and some other rapacious creatures, mammal and bird, often kills him on sight and only discovers afterwards that he has got a shrew instead of a mouse.

The mole is not universal; indeed on many hills no traces of him are to be seen, but he is common nevertheless, and on some of the high South Downs exceedingly abundant. Seeing him so numerous at the very highest points—the summit of Ditchling Hill and the long ridge extending from Ditchling Beacon to Mount Blackcap—the thought came into my mind that the moles were not like the birds and like myself, merely visitors on these heights, but old residents, and that their colonies had doubtless existed for scores and for centuries of years. And yet how could this be, since there is no water? For we have been taught to believe that the mole is a thirsty creature, that he must drink often, or at regular intervals, and drink deeply; and that to satisfy this want he makes runs to the nearest watercourse, that when there is no stream or pond near he sinks a well. Here there are no water-courses, and the dew ponds, few and far between, were all dried up during the excessively hot summer of 1899. The mole could not possibly sink a well in that hard chalk. Even human beings cannot do it. The few cottages that exist in this neighbourhood have no wells. The cottagers depend on the rain-water they catch and store, and when this is consumed in summer they have to go a distance of three or four miles for a supply. Yet here on the highest point, nearly a thousand feet above the flat country of the weald, the nearest place where it would be possible for them to obtain water, with nothing but the thin crust of soil above the hard chalk for them to live and move in, the moles were most abundant and active during the hot dry summer months.

One hot July morning, about ten o'clock, I was standing on Ditchling Hill looking at the hundreds of fresh mounds which the moles had been throwing up, and finding that they were still at work, it suddenly struck me that it would be a good plan to capture one of the industrious little beggars to ask him to tell me the secret of his presence in that waterless land. It is always best to go to the fountain-head for information. After a little watching I detected a movement in the loose earth in the last mound of a long row of hills marking the course of a new run. Placing myself over the mound I waited till it stirred again, then plunged my hand into the loose earth and grabbed at the little beast, but he slipped like quicksilver out of my hand and was gone. I very soon found another mole at work throwing up earth a foot or so in advance of a chain of seventeen hills of fresh dark mould all in a line. Altering my simple tactics, I thrust the point of my stick into the sod a few inches back from the point where he was working, and so cut off his retreat, and then caught and pulled him out. I have, first and last, interviewed a good many moles and know their disposition pretty well, but the extreme excitability and violence of this mole of the high downs fairly surprised me. Taking him to a spot where there was a smooth, close, hard turf, I released him, when, finding that he could not break through the matted roots and bury himself in the soil, he began to act in the maddest way, wriggling his body and dashing himself on the ground, screaming all the time as if someone was murdering him, although I was not touching nor even standing very near him. It was useless to interrogate so irrational a creature; and leaving him to make his way back to his own subterranean city, or Welbeck Abbey, I walked on still occupied with my mole problem. I could not suppose that want of water had made this individual mad, seeing that he was sleek and well-nourished and had struggled powerfully when I had held him in my hand. If I, so much bigger than a mole, had his strength and shape I could move mountains.

Walking on I met an intelligent-looking shepherd, who was, I found, a good observer and something of a naturalist; and to him I put the question that occupied me. He told me that he had been shepherding on these hills above forty years, and the moles had always been there where they had no water to drink. "They must drink or die, " said I: "it is down in the books, and therefore it must be true. " He shook his head at the books and replied that the moles come out at night to lick the grass—the dew was enough for them. "If that is so, " I said, "then they must die of thirst in seasons when there is no dew. " "They *do* die, " he answered; "in very dry windy summers, when there is no dew, you find a good many moles lying about dead on these hills every morning. " He added that they did not all die; that a year or so after a time of great mortality they became numerous again.

The story I had heard of the moles dying in numbers when there was no moisture to be got from the grass was afterwards confirmed by other persons whom I questioned on the subject—some of them shepherds, and some men of other occupations whose lives had been passed among the downs. Yet I could not say that the books are entirely wrong in what they tell us: it is a fact, I believe, that in lowlands where access to the water is easy moles do drink at regular intervals, and must drink to live; and we may believe that the hill-top moles in the course of long centuries, probably thousands of years, have become inured to other conditions, and, like many mammals found in waterless deserts, are able to exist without drinking. Moles transplanted from the lowlands would doubtless quickly perish on these hills.

When we come to the bird life of the downs we find that the species are not many. Nevertheless, there is more to be said about the birds than the mammals of this district, and much that I have to say about them must be reserved for other chapters. It may be said, without injustice, that Sussex has distinguished itself above all counties, with perhaps the exception of Norfolk, in the large number of native species it has succeeded in extirpating during the present century. >From its forest and heath lands, its marshes and shingled flats, its cliffs and downs, the following species among others of less account have disappeared: the raven, kite, common buzzard and honey buzzard, hen harrier and Montagu's harrier: of shore birds and terns, several species: bittern and reed pheasant, bustard, stone curlew, blackcock, chough, guillemot, razor-bill, kittiwake, and shag. Augustus Hare, in his lately-published work *Sussex*, speaks of Beachy Head as a haunt of thousands of sea-fowl—puffins, sea-gulls, choughs, etc. Bless the man! he is many years behind the times. On all the fifteen miles of precipitous chalk cliffs extending from Beachy Head to Brighton the only birds to be seen now are those commonest universal cliff-breeders, the herring-gull and jackdaw, and a few kestrels. The one surviving pair of peregrine falcons that haunt this coast have in recent years been annually robbed of their eggs or young.

It is not possible, said to me a gentleman residing on this south coast a year or two ago, for any man to see a large rare bird and not "go for it. " The pleasure of shooting it is too great to be resisted, however sorry he may be that all these fine birds are being exterminated throughout the country. If he is not himself a collector he will be sure to have a friend or neighbour who is, and who will be delighted to have a Sussex-killed raven, spoonbill, honey buzzard, or stone curlew sent him as a present.

This he said to me in explanation of his motives in shooting a buzzard.

I will here quote a passage touching on the bird life of the South Downs, in the early years of this century, from M. A. Lower's account of the shepherd's life in his *Contributions to Literature* (London, 1854). "Here are, " Lower says, "the very words of one now dead, who had himself carried the shepherd's crook and worn the shepherd's greatcoat for many years on these hills ":

The life of a shepherd in my young days was not the same as it is now.... You very seldom see a shepherd's hut on our hills in these times, but formerly every shepherd had one. Sometimes it was a sort of cave dug in the side of a bank or link, and had large stones inside. It was commonly lined with heath or straw. The part above ground was covered with sods of turf, or heath, or straw, or boughs of hawth. In rough, shuckish weather, the shepherd used to turn into his hut and lie by the hour together, only looking out once in a while to see that the sheep didn't stray too far. Here he was safe and dry, however the storm might blow overhead, and he could sit and amuse himself as he liked best. If he could read so much the better. It was in my hut, over in the next bottom to this, that I first read about

Moses and his shepherding life, and about David's killing of the lion and the bear. Ah, how glad I felt that we hadn't such wild beasties to frighten and maybe kill our sheep and us. The worst we ever had to fear were the foxes that sometimes killed a young lamb or two. But there was otherwhile a crueller than that. If a ewe happened to get overturned on a lonesome part of the hill the ravens and carrion crows would come and pick out her eyes before she was dead. This happened to two or three of my ewes, and at last I got an old gun and shot all the crows and ravens I could get nigh. Once I shot an eagle, but that was the only eagle I ever saw. Since the hills have been more broken by the plough such birds are but seldom seen. There haven't been any wild turkeys either for many a year. I have heard my father say he killed two or three no great while before I was born: they used to call them bustards. There used to be a good many buzzards on the hill when I was a boy. They did no hurt to the sheep, but they destroyed the game and the chickens. Once I set up a pair of clams for one in a thorn-bush in Box-holt Bottom, and when I went to look the next morning I found my bird catched by the legs. He was such a great fellow that I was afraid to tackle him, and was obliged to fetch him several raps over the head with my hook, which brought him sprawling, clams and all, to the ground, and I had a great to-do before I could kill him. Mottly Simmonds, a shepherd's boy that I once knew, put a long bit of string with a running knot to it round a buzzard's nest that he'd found in the hawth upon Norton Top, and when he saw her a-coming he got ready, and as soon as she was settled he pulled the string and catched her round both legs.

Old men of eighty or more who have shepherded on these downs may still remember when buzzards occasionally built their nests on a hawth or furze bush; to others it sounds like a story of ancient times, a picture of wild-bird life of the days when great bustards roamed in flocks on the downs and white spoonbills nested on the trees of West Dean, near Chichester.

The extermination of the black grouse is even more recent. The Rev. Edward Turner, in a paper printed in the *Sussex Archaeological Collections*, Vol. XIV. p. 62, writes as follows:

Ashdown Forest was well stocked with black game. So numerous were these birds at the commencement of the present century that it was hardly possible to ride or walk about it in any direction without disturbing some of them. At that time the forest was thickly covered with heath, but since then this has been so generally cut and carried away that the black game, deprived of the food and shelter they so much delight in, have gradually disappeared, and in this locality are now very rarely to be met with. This is to be deplored, for an old blackcock, with his forked tail and glossy sable plumage, is one of the finest of the British birds.

Of the species that have been extirpated on the downs, just now one is inclined to most keenly regret the stone curlew, not only because it is a fine big bird, singularly interesting in its habits, and possessing a powerful wild cry to gladden the souls of those who hear it, but also because its loss is so recent. In the early part of the century it was quite common on the downs, and bred on all the barren stony spots on the highest hills, as well as on the extensive shingly flats on the Pevensey coast. In spite of incessant persecution it clung to its ancient southern haunt, and succeeded each year in rearing a few young down to about twenty-five to thirty years ago. The shepherds knew it well, and the old and middle-aged men among them have many stories of their own experiences in hunting for its two stone-coloured eggs in the flinty places. During the last quarter of a century it has trembled on the verge of extinction, and I think I can say with truth that it is now, like the great bustard, nothing but a memory. One pair bred not far from Chanc-tonbury Ring about four or five years ago. In the spring of 1897 another pair bred on a down south of the village of Jevington, and the eggs were found by a shepherd and given by him to "the young squire, " the landlord's son, for his collection. In July this year (1899) I disturbed a stone curlew on the same down; a solitary bird, probably a survivor of the pair that tried to breed here two years before, revisiting his old home. And perhaps that wild yet human-like whistle it uttered in my hearing was its last farewell to downland.

It will be news to most naturalists that the long-eared owl frequented and probably bred in the thorn, holly, and furze patches among the South Downs until recently. I had this from the same observant shepherd who enlightened me about the moles, and the information came out incidentally. He was telling me of some curious experiences and of curious things he had seen during the long years of his shepherding on these hills; and related that about fifteen years ago a ewe in his flock dropped a lamb which had a round flat face with two round staring eyes set close together in the middle of it, and a nose coming to a sharp point, and bent downward like a hooked beak. The lamb appeared healthy and strong at birth, but it could not suck, its mouth being tightly closed, and in a day or two it died. Its resemblance to an owl in its face, he said, was quite wonderful; and it was his belief that the ewe when feeding among the furze had come upon an owl sitting in the middle of a bush, and the shock of suddenly seeing its round face and staring eyes had caused that deformed owlish countenance in the lamb.

His story did not surprise me, although monstrosities of that kind, which are the result of what my friend Mr. Frederic W. H. Myers has called (in the human subject) "pre-natal suggestion, " are comparatively rare among the lower animals. My belief is that they are very much more frequent among domestic than among wild animals, and that they are more common than we think. Not one case in a hundred is ever heard of, and when we do hear of one we are satisfied to classify it as a "freak of nature. " This, however, does not explain the fact that a cow, or sheep, or cat, or some other creature, will occasionally produce an offspring in the likeness of another very different animal. This same shepherd had another case in his flock. This was of a lamb clothed in a brown fur instead of wool—the fur, in fact, of a hare; and his belief was that the ewe, when pregnant, had been frightened by a hare suddenly jumping out of the heather or bushes where it had been crouching.

What did surprise me was that this man, with only the light of nature to go by, had found the right interpretation of these strange cases. With regard to the first case, I asked him where on the downs could a sheep ever see an owl. He then told me that a good many owls had always inhabited the largest furze patches, and that he had seen the birds closely on a good many occasions in the summer months, and was quite sure that it was the long-eared owl. He had never flushed an owl of another species in the downs, but had occasionally seen a white owl at night or late in the evening. He believed that the long-eared owl had now forsaken the downs. But though he was so positive about his facts, I am still in doubt as to the species: our memories play strange trick's with all of us at times; and after all it may have been in the autumn months that the birds were seen, and that the species was the world-wandering short-eared owl.

The only comparatively big birds to be met with now among the downs are those very common species that visit the district more or less regularly to feed. Large numbers of rooks from the wooded lowlands and daws from the sea-cliffs have their favourite feeding-grounds on the sheep-walks. The black-headed and common gulls winter on the coasts, and wherever the land is tilled are seen following the plough in autumn and spring. The bigger herring-gull breeds on the cliffs, and may be seen flying over the downs every day throughout the year. Wood-pigeons, the kestrel, an occasional sparrow-hawk, and a few stray birds of other rarer species are also to be seen. In the valleys of the rivers Cuckmere, Ouse, and Arun, that cut through the range, herons from the Parham heronry are common. I have frequently seen as many as a dozen to twenty together in the autumn months. Pewits and a few redshanks breed in the valleys in spring.

I have said that the only sea-bird that now breeds on the cliffs along the southern edge of the South Downs is the herring-gull. Their most interesting colony is at Seaford Head, where I have observed them during the last three summers. At that spot they are not decreasing, and they have as neighbours a large number of jackdaws, and two or three pairs of kestrels. I have a suspicion that the hawks do not consider that their eggs and young are safe from attack by their big loud-voiced neighbours, as I occasionally see a kestrel rise and furiously buffet the gulls passing and repassing before its nest on the face of the cliff.

In the first week of June last I had the good fortune to see the gulls at this spot in a new and beautiful aspect. At the top of the cliff, where it is about four hundred feet high, a quantity of earth has fallen or crumbled away, leaving a gap about thirty to forty feet deep, and into this I crept and placed myself as near the edge as I could safely get. Lying there perfectly still, the birds, which had been flying up and down before me uttering their loud anxious cries, began to settle on all the near projecting pieces of chalk where they could watch me. By-and-by I had twenty-four of them all perched close to me, in pairs or small groups of three or four, some of them standing on the chalk where it was partly overgrown with patches of sea-pink, or thrift. The intense whiteness of the sunlit chalk and rosy red of the numerous flat little flowers gave a novel and very beautiful appearance to the birds. For they were very near, and quite motionless, though clamouring with open beaks and swollen throats, and all their colours were clearly visible—the white and tender pale grey of the plumage, the shining yellow eye and yellow beak, with its orange-red patch on the lower mandible, and the flesh-coloured legs.

It is interesting to watch the kestrel in summer, after his breeding season, hunting for food on the parched downs. He is most common on the high ridge on the northern border of the range, overlooking his woodland home on the flat country below. It strikes one as curious to see this bird haunting the same slopes day after day, flying about by the hour, pausing at intervals to hover motionless for a minute or so, then dashing down to seize his prey; for you know that no creature as big as the smallest baby mouse exists at the spot. The fact is, he is catching grasshoppers, which are abundant; and the wonder is that all this important strategy, these beautiful evolutions and display of wing-power, should be put in practice for such a purpose. The pipits and larks creeping on the surface capture and swallow their grasshoppers without any trouble. But the kestrel has but one method, and he cannot vary it; he must look for his quarry when at a height of sixty or seventy feet from the surface, even if it be a grasshopper; and must hover long as if to take a sure aim, and finally precipitate himself upon it with as much violence as he uses for a mouse or bird.

Another common bird of the downland is the turtle-dove. A shepherd told me that on the arrival of these birds last spring a flock of not less than five hundred fed every day for over a week in some fields at the foot of Mount Blackcap, near Lewes. The birds are certainly very abundant, and wherever there is a patch of large furze mixed with whitethorn and bramble bushes you find them breeding in numbers, their frail platform nests placed four or five feet above the ground out of reach of the foxes. It is pleasant to listen to their low monotonous crooning in these quiet solitary places.

In June the missel-thrushes, after rearing their young, forsake the woodlands and homesteads of the weald and the maritime district for the open downs, and are met with everywhere in small flocks of half a dozen to thirty or forty birds. During the sultry hours they keep close in the shelter of the furze and bramble bushes, and when disturbed rush violently out, emitting their harsh cry, and when flying away look almost white in the dazzling sunlight.

But the missel-thrush is a gipsy and rover at this season of the year in all the open treeless districts in the country. The small breeding species characteristic of the furze-clad downs are the common bunting and yellowhammer, the whitethroat, dun-nock, meadow pipit, stonechat, and whinchat. Most of these vanish at the approach of winter, some to seek other climes, and others, the dunnock included, to spend the cold months in sheltered situations in the lowlands.

A few birds of the woods and homesteads also come in summer to the solitary furze-gardens—thrush and blackbird, robin, wren, and chaffinch. And here too you find the red-backed shrike; but he is most common among the thorns at the foot, of the downs on the north side of the range. All these birds of the downs, I have said, inhabit and breed in the furze and other bushes. The skylark and wheatear are exceptions. The skylark is fairly common all over the hills, and breeds either in the corn-fields or on the untilled downs where they are covered with a thick grass which the sheep refuse to eat. The wheatear does not find many suitable breeding-places on the smooth turf of the sheep-walks; the barren, rough, stony places he loves best are few and far between. He usually lays his eggs in an old rabbit-hole on some spot where the chalk and flints are only partially covered by a scanty turf. At one spot very near the sea I found ten or twelve pairs breeding quite close together. And here again, as in the case of the gulls seen standing on and against the patches of rose-red sea-pink, I came upon a wonderful flower-and-bird scene and living picture of exquisite beauty, and saw the pretty wheatear as I had never seen him before, and most probably shall never see him again. The birds were breeding near the top of a high down where it sloped or dropped very abruptly to the valley below. It was a rough flinty place, honeycombed with rabbit-holes, and thickly grown over with big sea-poppy plants in full blossom. Lying coiled up in a hollow of the ground I had this garden of poppies, which covered about half an acre of ground, all round and above me, and looking up, the higher graceful grey plants, blossom-crowned, were seen against the sky. The great flower, as I then saw it for the first time, its purest yellow made luminous and brilliant with the sunlight streaming through it, seen against the ethereal blue beyond, had a new unimaginable loveliness. The wheatears were all round me, some with grubs in their beaks, but not venturing to enter their nesting-holes, flitting from place to place; some remaining in one place to keep watch, others going and coming. But as time went on, and I still refused to stir, they grew tired of waiting, and of uttering their chacking alarm-note and flirting their pretty tails, and began carrying food into the burrows: two of these were within a dozen yards of my resting-place. But even after they had quieted down, at intervals one of the birds would rise up and suspend himself motionless in the air and watch me for some moments. Down at the foot of the hill below me some of the birds were to be seen hunting for insects on the lawn-like turf, and as they flew slowly over it, close to the surface, on rapidly beating wings, they had the appearance of great black-winged butterflies flitting across the green sward.

Near this colony, at a spot where there is a good deal of furze, I observed that the wheatear, like some small birds of the woodland, is a great hater of the red-backed shrike. When attacking he hovers like a kestrel at a height of eight or ten yards above his enemy, then dashes down upon him and finally chases him away. It is not very probable that young wheatears are often or ever attacked by the shrike; but this pretty little bird looks what he is—a butcher among birds; and besides, the wheatear has doubtless seen him attack the young of other species, and slay them with his hawk-like beak.

A few notes on the reptiles of the downs will conclude this long chapter on wild life.

The common lizard is found everywhere among the gorse and heath, but is not so abundant as in suitable localities in the lowlands. Everyone is familiar with the debilitating or paralysing effect produced on rabbits and hares by a stoat when he hunts them; and we are familiar, too, with a similar weakness in the frog when pursued by a snake. But it is not known that our common little lizard suffers in the same way. I do not see how any snake, even the swift-moving smooth snake that preys almost exclusively on that creature, could ever catch lizards if they were not subject to this singular infirmity. But the lizard is not so easily overcome with terror, or hypnotised, if anyone prefers that word, as the frog; nor does he appear so weak on the high downs as I have found him on the heaths of Hampshire and Surrey. He is so alert, and quick to vanish into cover at the slightest alarm, that it is not nearly so easy to experiment with the lizard as it is with the frog. It is in fact exceedingly difficult, and fifty lizards may be found and not one will wait quietly to be experimented on. But my experience is that when a walking-stick is thrust snakewise through the grass or heath towards the basking lizard, he at once begins to suffer mysteriously in his brightness and vigour, and his efforts to escape become feebler while the hidden imaginary enemy steals after him. On the downs I found that the stick thrust towards the lizard in many instances did not produce the debilitating effect; but the little creature, instantly changing his habits, ran quickly to and up a bush. One that I had frightened with my stick amused me by emerging on the top of a furze bush, and sitting there, high as my breast, and safe from snakes as he perhaps thought, curiously eyed me with his bright bird-like little eyes.

This then is our alert and elusive little lizard's weakness, and though I have occasionally played on it for fun during the last two or three summers, I pitied him, and was almost sorry that I had found it out.

Once only in the South Downs have I seen the lizard's worst enemy, the smooth snake. He is like the creature he pursues, alert and quick to escape, and may not be quite so rare as we imagine.

The adder is common in suitable places, on the high slopes, especially where the gorse bushes grow mixed with heath and tussocky grass. In some spots they are no doubt very numerous, as a good many sheep die of adder's bite. Occasionally a sheep is bitten in the side, and one can only suppose in such cases that the animal has lain down on a very sluggish adder basking in the sun at the side of a furze bush. But most of the victims are bitten on the nose. Sheep, I believe, have no instinctive fear of a serpent; and they are always curious about any odd-looking object they see, and will go out of their way to smell at and touch it with their nose: it is not strange that they occasionally get killed.

I see fewer adders by chance, and am less successful in finding when I look for them, here than in some favourite haunts in other southern counties, simply because I go to the downs in summer and not in early spring. Those who are familiar with the adder, and occasionally look for and find him, know that he is most easily found and oftenest seen by chance when the year is young. This is not because after his winter sleep he is still dull of sense, slow to move, and made drowsy or lethargic by the unaccustomed heat of the sun. In early spring he is on the contrary more alert, more sensitive to the earth-tremors that warn him of an approaching danger, than at any later period. It is certain, too, that the females, when heavy with young in June and July, are much less wary and quick to slip away than at other seasons.

In spring, especially in March, when winter is still in the air, the adder must find a sheltered spot looking towards the sun; and whether on a bank, or at the side of a furze or bramble bush, or on the lower part of any sloping ground, the young spring grass, or the old pale dead grass and leaves of last year, serve to show him up. Once your eye has caught and distinguished his form, it looks strangely conspicuous—a something separate from the vegetation it rests upon. He is like a richly-coloured or brightly-embroidered garter, or ribbon, dropped by chance on the pale colourless ground.

Seeing him thus, looking so startlingly bright, so separate from his surroundings, one is apt to imagine that careful Mother Nature has not been so careful of her adder as she has of most of her other weak and persecuted children. At this early season the adder's only protection is his alertness and shy habit.

In summer the case is different, when in place of the young fresh grass and the pale neutral ground-tints that make him so conspicuous, thare is a rough surface and a rich and various colouring; and though not invisible he is not easily distinguishable. On hot days he does not lie exposed to the sun, but prefers to rest where grasses and herbage, mixed perhaps with the feathery foliage of the lower branches of a bush, shot through and sprinkled and spotted with shifting sunlight and shadow, make up a broken picture, the numberless minute details of which you cannot see separately. If, on such a variegated ground, you are able to detect and closely regard without alarming him, you will be rewarded with a very beautiful sight. You will see that his ground-colour, whatever the precise tint may be, from pale yellow or palest brown, to a copper or terra-cotta red, assimilates to the colour of the soil, and to the stems and leaves of ripe grasses; and that the sand in the earth, the seeding grasses, and scaly coil, sparkle alike at each point where a sunbeam touches them. The zigzag band, too, fits in with the shadows, and is not easily distinguishable from the dark wavering lines and spots and blotches made by twigs and leaves that intercept the sunlight.

The adders of the downs are not so varied in colour as in the New Forest, and in most cases have a light yellowish ground-colour with an intense black mark. Some beautiful varieties are, however, to be seen. Last summer a shepherd described to me one he had killed as a very pretty creature, with a bright chestnut-red zigzag band on a whitish body.

At a dinner-table at a village in the downs where I was staying, I once found it necessary to explain to the others that it did not make me miserable to be out all day, and on most days alone, on the downs. It was, I assured them, a constant pleasure to see the beautiful creatures there—the birds, the adder, the fox, and others. After a long silence, a man sitting opposite to me said, "Excuse me, sir, but did I understand you to say that you consider the adder a beautiful creature? " I replied in the affirmative, and after another interval of silence he laid down his knife and fork and delivered himself as follows: "Well, that I can't understand. An adder is an adder, and there's no doubt about what a man feels when he sees it. I have never heard anyone till this moment say the contrary. Most people kill an adder when they find one. I don't. When I suddenly see an adder before me when I am out walking or riding, and stop still, and he gives me a look out of his eyes, and I see that he is just getting ready to fly at me, I don't stop to kill him. I'm off. You call that a beautiful creature—-"

This is one and a somewhat extreme view of the adder's character. But it comes nearest to the popular feeling about that creature whose power to harm us we so greatly exaggerate. Here is a case which presents us with the opposite extreme. A gentleman of Bognor, Mr. W. H. B. Fletcher, occasionally amuses himself by taming adders, which he takes with a butterfly net on the downs. He is accustomed to pick up his tame adders by the handful—six or seven at a time, all wriggling and winding round and among his open fingers; and he affirms that after an adder has been four or five days in his keeping it becomes so tame that it may be handled with impunity—by Mr. Fletcher. In fact, his serpents are of so gentle a disposition that he doubts if it would be possible to tease them into an attempt to bite him. He has shown me a collection of photographs, of his hand grasping a bunch of adders, not to be hurled in anger and with deadly effect at his enemies, but picked up simply to show what exceedingly mild and sweet-tempered creatures they are when you trust them and they are accustomed to a human hand. Now it is common knowledge that some persons possess a quality, or energy, which enables them to handle the most irritable and venomous reptiles with safety: a touch of their hand, and, in some extreme cases, their mere presence, will soothe and make them harmless. I do not say that it is so in this case. Mr. Fletcher laughs at such an explanation of his power, and says that he would not venture to pick up wild adders by their tails, as I sometimes do. His adders are savage at first, but in a very short time grow accustomed to the hand, and may then be taken up and handled by any person. Dr. Giinther says he has met with cases similar to the one I have related; and he tells of a gentleman who, to show how harmless the tamed adder can be made, is accustomed to put one into the hands of his little child.

The ring-snake, though found in the valleys, is exceedingly rare on the high downs. But the snake compared with the adder is a great traveller, and he is sometimes met with miles away from the low meadows and pasture lands where the frog abides; and I will conclude this chapter with a strange story of a big snake found by a shepherd-boy on one of the highest points of the South Downs, between the villages of Jevington and Willingdon. He was an intelligent boy of thirteen, and finding him in a lonely spot with his flock I stopped to have a chat with him, and he was delighted to talk about the small birds, the foxes, rabbits, adders, and other inhabitants of the furze bushes known to him. After some talk I said good-bye and went on; but had not walked fifty yards before he came running after me, to say that he had forgotten to tell me about the big snake. One day last summer he was with his flock near a wheat-field, and in the corn he found a skylark's nest, with five young birds in it. In the evening he told two of his playmates about the nest; and next day they all went together to visit it, and agreed to take the young birds home and bring them up in cages; and as young larks usually die when taken small they planned to leave them in the nest until they were grown and almost ready to fly. When the proper time came, and the birds were nearly ready to make their escape, they went to the field with a cage; but on arriving at the spot found the nest empty, and a huge snake lying coiled up near it. When they discovered it they were very much afraid, owing to its great size and threatening aspect, as it rose up and hissed loudly at them. But it moved away very slowly, hindered, like the famous serpent of Horsham, by "a quantity of thickness in the middle. " Arming themselves with big flints, they began to stone it, and one sharp flint striking it with great force cut its body open, when, from the wound, out fell one of the full-grown young larks. When they had finished killing the snake, and pressed its body where the thickness was with their feet, the other four birds were forced out. They took the snake home, and all the people in the village came to look at it, hanging to the branch of a tree; and the schoolmaster measured it with a foot-rule, and found that it was exactly four feet in length. Its body, the boy said, was as thick as his arm.

There was nothing incredible in his story. There are well-authenticated cases, of much bigger snakes, some six feet long, killed in England. Last summer I caught and measured four snakes in the New Forest, and the two biggest were three feet, and three feet one inch, respectively. If these snakes had been killed they would probably have measured more, as it is exceedingly difficult to get the proper length when they are violently struggling to free themselves, and contracting their bodies; but I should have been very sorry to kill one even to add several inches to its three feet.

CHAPTER VI

THE SHEPHERD OF THE DOWNS

The shepherd as a picturesque figure—His best qualities racial—The Saxon type predominant in downland—The peasant's good looks—A great beer-drinker—Scene in a village public-house—Bad and good qualities of the peasant—Character in a small boy—Beauty of person—A labourer's family—A pet lamb and the Salvation Army—A Sussex maid—Persistence of type—The Culpepper family—The shepherd's good looks—Contented minds—A talk with a shepherd.

That solitary cloaked figure on the vast round hill, standing motionless, crook in hand, and rough-haired dog at heel, sharply seen against the clear pale sky, is one of those rare human forms in this land, which do not ever seem out of place in the landscape. It is undoubtedly a form to attract and fascinate the eye. But behind the seeing eyes are the differing busy minds. There are those, for instance, who are interested solely in the image, the semblance; who are not, like the fox in the fable, concerned as to what is inside of a pretty head, but who look on living faces and forms as on carvings and sculptures in a gallery. Then, again, there are those who perpetually crave to get at the human heart in any human figure; who will go on pushing down or peeping behind screen after screen, and are never satisfied until they have seen behind the last screen of all. I am not sure if these were to follow the downland shepherd to his lowly home, to converse familiarly every day and live intimately with him, that they would not be disappointed, and conclude that the differences between him and others of his rank and race, who have other occupations—the labour of the weald, for instance—are very much on the surface and hardly worth troubling about.

I class myself somewhere between the two extremes: not satisfied with the mere semblance or appearance of things, seeing men as trees and rocks, or as works of art, I am nevertheless not teased— "tormented, " De Quincey would have written—with that restless desire to pry into and minutely examine the secret colour and texture of the mind of every person I meet. It is the mental attitude of the naturalist, whose proper study is not mankind but animals, including man; who does not wish to worry his brains overmuch, and likes to see very many things with vision a little clearer than the ordinary, rather than to see a very few things with preternatural clearness and miss all the rest.

In the case of the downland shepherd, this comparatively superficial knowledge which contents me has made me greatly admire him. That he differs considerably from others on the surface we cannot but see; and it would indeed seem strange if this had not been the case, since the conditions of his life are and have been for generations unlike those of other peasants; still, his best and sterling qualities are undoubtedly of the race. Probably the villagers of the downs and the weald of Sussex have more Saxon blood in their veins than the people of any other part of England: at all events it may, I think, be said that the Saxon characteristics, physical and moral, predominate in them. Many of the coast people, those especially who are seafarers, are markedly of Danish descent: away from the sea the Saxon type is commonest; the round, rosy face, steady, sometimes hard blue eyes, and light brown hair. Red and yellow hair, too, is very common—every shade from the pale reddish yellow miscalled "ginger, " to the intense colour miscalled "carroty, " and the beautiful "auburn" and "Venetian" reds.

They are a good-looking people, and good to live with, though I do not admire, or perhaps it would be better to say love, them as much as I do the people of Somerset. It is probably due to the Celtic blood in the peasants of that county that gives their women a softness and sweetness exceeding that of other counties, a more delicate red colour when they are young. But the Sussexians, though perhaps not the best, nor the most lovable, are quite good enough, and are, I believe, the strongest and hardiest in Southern England. They may also be described as fairly sober, although they drink a good deal— more perhaps than the people of any other southern county; but they have remarkably steady heads and carry their liquor well. It is true that you will generally find a few topers at the village inn, boozing at all hours of the day, but that you will find all the country over; and it will always be the same so long as publicans are permitted by the authorities to serve habitual topers and half-drunk men generally with liquor. We know that the public-houses are now all tied, and tied very strictly, and if the publican does not sell as much beer as the villagers, drunk or sober, are anxious to drink, he must turn out and give place to someone with a better sense of what is due to the brewer.

I was much amused one morning at a drinking scene I witnessed in the village public at East Dean. It was only eleven o'clock, but in the bar-room I found six men, who had evidently been there drinking a long time, each with a tall blue mug of beer at his side. Five of them were middle-aged—all over forty, I should say, and all Saxons with hard red faces and hard blue eyes. These were men who could drink gallons of beer, then walk very steadily home; only a slight wavering in their eyes when they looked at me told that they had been a long time busy with their blue mugs. But the sixth was a young man of a different type: he had not the breadth and depth of chest of the others, and his eyes and hair were dark and his face pale. And he was pretty drunk. The talk, after ranging over a variety of subjects, was finally all about getting up early in the morning to go to work, and the degree of reluctance each man felt at the necessity of turning out of bed. On this subject the young and tipsy man spoke feelingly, and was almost eloquent. He said that with him it generally depended on how much beer he had drunk the previous day: if he had drunk a good deal, then he woke with such a bad head and such a weight on him that to turn out was a positive torture, and he was miserable all day long. He believed, he added, that it must be pretty much the same with everybody.

No one answered him a word; he was touching on delicate ground. But their silence piqued him, and staring defiantly round he continued, "If you ask me, I'll tell you what my opinion really is. My opinion is that beer is the curse of the country. And when I say that beer is the curse of the country I'm pretty blank well sure that I'm pretty blank well right. " And here, to emphasise his expression of opinion, which had not perhaps been strong enough to satisfy him, he banged his fist on the deal table at which he sat, and in doing so accidentally capsized his tall blue mug, and sent the contents streaming all over the wood. Picking up the mug he rapped loudly on the table with it, and when the publican came from an inner room ordered him to wipe up the spilt beer and fill his mug again.

Consistent young man! The others gazed at him with grave disapproval in their blue not quite steady eyes, but said nothing. His sentiments were no doubt regarded as most unnatural, his words as flat treason to their order. They did not consider, or did not know, that their order in another larger sense was not his; that they were distant children of those who came with Ella to these purple shores, abandoned by Rome; that they had not so greatly degenerated in fourteen centuries as not to be able to drink any dark-eyed and pale-faced young man into the deepest depths of intoxication, or the grave, without themselves experiencing a qualm, physical or mental.

Putting aside the subject of drink, perhaps the two greatest faults of this people (and too much beer may be the reason of both) is that they are not very thrifty and not very pure. In some of the villages illegitimate children are as plentiful as blackberries. But altogether, the good qualities are more and greater than the vices, or "amiable weaknesses"; and no person can help admiring their rock-like stability of character, their sturdy independence of spirit, and, with it, patient contentment with a life of unremitting toil; and, finally, their intense individuality. You will recognise even in the children these strong enduring qualities, which make the Sussexian peasant a man "self-centred as the trees and animals are. " Here is an account of a conversation I had with a little fellow, under nine, at a village on the northern border of the downs. At sunset on a misty autumn evening I set out to walk to a spot about three miles from the village. The children had just been released from school, and I overtook a group of them going my way in a lane a little distance from the village. Not being quite sure of the way I asked them to direct me; but they were too eager to help, and the short cuts they recommended across fields and commons, and through woods, with turnings this way and that way, and numerous other details, only served to confuse me, and saying that it was no good I walked on. Then the small rosy, round-faced, blue-eyed boy said he was going a couple of miles my way and would show me how to get to my place.

Before we had gone many yards a grey mist came over and obscured the scene. It was getting dark, too, and I remarked to the little fellow that the days would be shorter still by-and-by, and that it would be very dark and lonely for him after school hours. He replied that he knew the way well across the fields and common, and by the lanes, and he was not afraid of the dark. Not when it is quite black, I asked, and raining or snowing? No, he said, however dark it was he could not lose his way, and he didn't mind the rain in the least. He had a good coat for winter, and good boots. Here he asked me to stop and look at his boots. He had another nicer pair for Sunday wear. Then he gave me a description of all his possessions in the way of garments; but the winter coat which his mother had made for him was the possession he valued most. I asked him if his father worked on a farm. No, he said, his father had left home a long time ago and would never return. Perhaps he had gone to some other country: he did not know where he was, and never expected to see him again. Bit by bit he told me more of his story. There were two—himself, not nine, and a little brother, too little to go to school. They lived with a woman who took care of them in a cottage a couple of miles from the village. His mother, left to provide for herself and children, had gone into service at Brighton. She worked very hard and kept them well clothed. He would see her at Christmas, and be with her a whole week; that would be a happy time. Then I remarked tentatively, "I suppose it was drink that caused the trouble. " "Oh, no, " he returned quickly; "father did not drink—he was not a man of that sort. Father was not a bad man. I should like to see him again, but he will never come back. " Then I said, determined to get at the bottom of the affair: "If your father was not bad, and loved his children, why did he go away and throw this burden on your poor mother and cause all this sorrow? " He was silent for a few moments, and then, with all the gravity in the world, he replied, "It was an upset, " and beyond that not one word would he say. If I had given him silver and gold, it would not have unlocked his firm little lips.

That little word *upset* is an exceedingly useful one in the peasant's limited vocabulary, and covers a great variety of domestic infelicities in which the passion of anger plays a part, from the trivial disagreements between husband and wife which will be forgotten before the sun sets, to the tragedy that severs all sacred ties and will be a bitterness in the heart to the very end of life.

From what I have said so far it will appear that strength rather than grace and beauty is the principal characteristic of this people. But beauty we know is everywhere: and I do not now mean that beauty which is inherent in all human beings, in all things, for those who have eyes to see it, but beauty in the ordinary sense, visible to all, the lustre that is like genius, and springs up we know not how nor why in the most unpromising places. Beauty and grace and sweetness and melody—you will find them here, too, in the shadow of the downs, although not so frequently as in the sweet west country. Still, my experience is that the fair to see, and the pleasant and gracious, and the graceful in mind and manner, are not very rare.

It was my experience at a small downland village, where I desired to spend a few days, to find on arrival that, besides the inn where I wished not to go, there was but one cottage in the place in which it would be possible to get a lodging, and in this chance cottage to meet the sweetest people of their class I have ever stayed with in any village in England. And I have visited many villages and stayed in many cottages.

It chanced that a number of persons who had no home in the neighbourhood had found occupation in the village, and some of them, eight or nine I think, had received accommodation at this place. Hearing that the house was full I was not very confident of getting a bed; but when I came and looked at the place, and passed into the peaceful shadows of its grey walls and ancient trees, and when I knocked at the door under the porch, and it was opened to me by a comely young woman with the softest dark eyes and soft and most musical voice, I begged her not to refuse me and make me walk miles away in that blazing sun when I was tired and hungry and wanted food and rest. She considered the matter for some moments, then asked me in to dinner, for it was the dinner-hour; and later in the day some good-natured fellow was persuaded to give up his room to me and accept a shake-down in another part of the house.

The place really was a house, although let at a cottage rental to a working-man. It was a very old farmhouse, deprived of its land and standing apart in its own grounds, with large shade-trees in front and an orchard behind. There were many rooms, low-ceilinged and scantily furnished, and an immense old kitchen with a brick floor. The charm of the place was outside, where for long years Nature had had a free hand to make it beautiful in her own matchless way. The rough stone walls and low-tiled roof were overgrown with ivy, and small creepers, and grey and yellow lichen and stone-crop; and all the orchard and the ground that had once been garden was covered with grass and with wild flowers and garden flowers—wallflower, periwinkle, marigold, and others—run wild.

The tenant was a giant of a man with the hugest hands and immense long hairy arms like a gorilla, and a head that looked as if it had been roughly hewn out of some great black rock. Big and rough and dark, he looked almost dangerous, and I wondered how he had won that very gentle pretty woman to be his wife. But "something had come into his heart, " perhaps, to alter its nature and make him in disposition like herself. He was like a good, preternaturally grave, child, and being inarticulate he seldom opened his mouth. I remember one hot afternoon when we were at tea his sudden appearance in the doorway, and how, leaning on the doorframe looking in and down upon us, tired and black and dusty, his shirtsleeves rolled up displaying his huge hairy arms, he seemed like some strange half-human monster who had just come up out of the interior of the earth, where he had been occupied blowing the bellows for Vulcan, or on some such huge grimy task. His wife cast a glance at him, and after a little while, and with just the faint suspicion of a smile playing about her mouth, she remarked, "Look at Old Blackie! " It was plain to anyone who could read the feeling in the expression and the voice that she loved her rough giant.

She was helped in the housework by a sister, a nice-looking girl of nineteen, and there were two little children, perfect little Saxons with round rosy faces, light hair, and blue eyes, as unlike their parents in appearance as they were in their indomitable little tempers. But they were pretty, delightful children for all that.

Besides the people of the house there were four unhuman inmates— a semi-domestic robin who visited the kitchen at all hours; a tabby cat who was perpetually being dragged hither and thither by the two little ones, and bore it all with singular equanimity; a very old good-tempered collie dog, and a pet lamb. The lamb was often tethered in the orchard to keep him out of mischief, and whenever I went near him he would look to me for a biscuit or a lump of sugar, and failing to get it he would try to eat my clothes. It was on account of this animal that I found out something of the inner life of the people of the house which I should not otherwise have known. I told my gentle hostess that her lamb was not quite happy left alone tied up in the orchard, and I wondered that they, poor hard-working people, had burdened themselves with so unsuitable an animal for a pet.

She said that the lamb was not intended to be kept as a pet; they had it for another purpose, and what that purpose was I easily drew from her and her husband.

They were religious people, and had always been "church, " as their parents and grandparents had been before them, but now for a very long time past the church had been growing less and less to them, until they had ceased to attend it, although there was no chapel there and they had joined no other sect. The only reason of this estrangement appeared to be that their pastor was not a spiritual-minded man, and though a good many years vicar in a small parish, he did not even know his own parishioners, and was wholly occupied with his own mundane affairs and amusements. Now it is just as hard, nay impossible, for the ordinary Christian to live his ideal life apart from teachers and fellow-disciples as for a sheep left behind by the flock, and lost or abandoned by the shepherd, to exist by itself on the hills. And these two, feeling the great want in their lives, had allowed their hearts and hopes to go out to the Salvation Army. There would be no coldness nor want of guidance and encouragement in that fold! It was not their wish to put on a distinctive garb, nor in any way to make themselves conspicuous in a place where there was no—what shall I say—*barracks*, but to continue to live their own lives in the old way in their remote village, only feeling that there was a bond between them and other servants of their Master, that they were not alone. Thus far had they got when they heard that a great meeting of the Army was about to take place at the Crystal Palace—a jubilee or important celebration of some kind, at which the world-wandering General himself would be present to preside over a gathering of people from all parts of the kingdom, and from all the kingdoms of the earth. They resolved that the husband should attend the meeting, and in due time, having got permission from his master, he journeyed up to London, and after an absence of two or three days he returned with heart and mind full of the wonderful things he had witnessed. She had never been to London, and had never seen a big crowd; but little by little, taking up the disjointed bits of information that fell from him at odd times, and piecing them together, she had succeeded in forming a fairly accurate though somewhat vague mental picture of the scene. It was a vast palace of glass, filled with an excited multitude that no man could number. People were there from all countries, all regions of the earth; and black and yellow and red skins were seen among the white; and some of these people were in strange garments of bright colours, such as the heathen wear. And there was a great noise of prayer and praise and of countless musical instruments, and cries of joy and of shouting Hosannah to the Lord. Most wonderful was it to see how one feeling, one spirit, animated all alike, that in all those thousands upon thousands there was no eye that was not wet with tears and no face that did not shine with a divine passion of love and joy.

When she had finished the story, he, the silent man, added, "I can't say what I felt, but when I saw it all I could only say, 'If Heaven is like this, then it must be a good place to be in. '" Could he have said more?

After that great event it was planned that the wife should go up to the next annual gathering of the Army, and that like very many others of its friends she should take some little gift or thank-offering; and after many days' discussion it was settled that, as they lived in the South Downs, a lamb would be the most appropriate gift to offer. Money was put by for the purpose, and a young lamb bought at a neighbouring farm and reared by hand so as to make it very tame. It would, they thought, look so well in a procession of gift-bearers, its fleece washed white as snow, its neck decorated with bright ribbons and flowers, its mistress leading it by a silken cord.

I had forgotten all about the lamb, and was not too delighted to hear of the glorious future that awaited it. No doubt it would look very pretty in its snowy fleece, blue ribbons and flowers, led by its gentle, dove-eyed mistress; but close behind her and her singing fellow-processionists I could see as in a vision the Salvation butcher in his red waistcoat, keeping time to the music while sharpening a big broad-bladed knife on a screaming steel.

But it was idle to vex my mind about the ultimate destiny of an animal created for man's use. I daresay that even that famous lamb that was accustomed to attend Mary in all her walks had its throat cut in the end, and was very much relished, with mint sauce, by the worthy persons who ate it.

To return to the good people whose simple faith and lovable disposition was a refreshment to my soul. How they worked and how they dreamed, looking forward to the day that would be more than any other day in the year! By five in the morning the good man was away to his work, and any time from six to seven I could count on getting a cup of tea in the kitchen. At nine we breakfasted: at one dined: at five had tea, and supped when we dropped in, at nine or ten o'clock. The hour of eleven found us often still at table, and our poor host, who had been toiling all day in the blazing sun, would sometimes drop off over his supper. "Poor old Blackie has gone to sleep, " his wife would say, and leaning over and shaking his shoulder she would cry in his ear, "Wake up! " Then he would start and rub his drowsy eyes, and go on with his meal, and by-and-by she who had aroused him would drop her head; and he would lean over and shake her by the arm, and in turn cry, "Wake up! " It was often a merry time when we were together drinking our last cups of tea before tumbling tired to bed. Some would have preferred beer or something stronger, but it was curious to note how those two rare elements of personal charm and the subtle flame of religious feeling united in this woman, exercised a subduing and refining influence on that mixed crew in the house, and made even the most godless anxious to seem better than they were in her loved eyes.

Of the wife's sister, whom I have mentioned, one slight incident which impressed me at the moment remains to be told. She was utterly unlike her sister in her high bright colour, fluffy golden brown hair, blue-grey eyes, and perfect aquiline features. One evening she came in from the orchard, where she had been having a game of romps with the little children on the grass before putting them to bed, and to amuse them had pulled some slender sprays of small-leafed ivy and sewn them round the band of her cloth cap. Forgetting the garland, and flushed and merry, she came in and sat down opposite the west window, through which the level rays of the setting sun streamed full on her face. Looking at it, as it appeared in profile in that dim interior—the classical lines of the face and sunlit hair and ivy crown—the effect was as of something quite familiar and yet novel and never previously seen. It was in fact a face and head that we are all familiar with in art, now for the first time in my experience seen alive. I vaguely remembered, too, that once upon a time the old Romans had possessed an important settlement close by, perhaps at that very spot; and the thought came to me that perhaps long long centuries ago, one summer evening, a Roman maiden of nineteen came in from a merry game with her married sister's little ones on the grass, her shining hair crowned with ivy; and had sat down in some dim room among her people, just when the sun was going down behind the great downs, and poured its red light on her flushed, beautiful young face.

It pleased the girl to be told that she was like a Roman-British maid who had lived at that spot seventeen centuries ago; but she could not say that she had any but peasant's blood in her veins. Her parents and grandparents, and their families as far back as she knew, were all of the working class, and their home was the Sussex Downs. But the family memory seldom goes back far enough—it is rare for it to extend farther than three generations back. We see that racial characters are practically everlasting, that they are never wholly swamped. Families of distinct races may go on mixing and remixing their blood for scores of generations; yet children ever and anon will continue to be born that seem not the offspring of their parents, or of any near progenitors; but in them the ancient type that was obscured and appeared about to be lost for ever is suddenly restored, distinct in all its lineaments. It is as if a cask of soured and turbid liquor, in some day of strange atmospheric conditions, had suddenly run clear again, and had again the lost fragrance and flavour, and sparkle and brilliant colour: and this is a miracle of nature, an eternal mystery, and is like a reincarnation and a resurrection.

As with racial characters, so it is, although in a less degree, with fixed family features, and with the characters, physical and moral, that are produced by what is called good blood. These features and characters may become obscured and even disappear for a time; but they are not lost; from generation to generation they will ever and anon continue to reappear. This well-known fact and the less familiar fact that a very large number of persons of good family are constantly being submerged in the lower ranks, is to my mind a sufficient and the only explanation of the numerous handsome and beautiful faces and figures to be found among the peasantry.

I here recall the case of the once-important and numerous Sussex family of Culpepper; a member of that family, the old herbalist, has made the name familiar to everyone. For centuries the Culpeppers were landowners in various parts of the county, and at one period there were two baronetcies in the family. Yet in the course of the last two centuries they have sunk into utter obscurity, and there is not now one person of that name in Sussex above the condition of a labourer.

Similar cases may be found in every part of the country: the point that concerns us here is that probably in no other part of Sussex, perhaps in no other part of the kingdom, has the process of sinking to the lower social level been so frequent as in down-land. Or perhaps it would be more correct to say, that nowhere else have the old families that have lost their position in the country left so many descendants who bear their names and are labourers on the lands that were once their ancestors'. Among those of his class in downland the shepherd appears to have the largest infusion of good blood: it shows itself in the fine and even noble features that are so frequently found among them, and a degree of intelligence beyond that of the average shepherd of other districts.

One of the numerous, mostly minute, differences to be detected between the downland shepherd and other peasants—differences due to the conditions of his life—refers to his disposition. He has a singularly placid mind, and is perfectly contented with his humble lot. In no other place have I been in England, even in the remotest villages and hamlets, where the rustics are not found to be more or less infected with the modern curse or virus of restlessness and dissatisfaction with their life. I have, first and last, conversed with a great many shepherds, from the lad whose shepherding has just begun to the patriarch who has held a crook, and "twitched his mantle blue, " in the old Corydon way, on these hills for upwards of sixty years, and in this respect have found them all very much of one mind. It is as if living alone with nature on these heights, breathing this pure atmosphere, the contagion had not reached them, or else that their blood was proof against such a malady.

One day I met a young shepherd on the highest part of the South Downs, who was about twenty-three years old, handsome, tall, well-formed, his face glowing with health and spirits. I shared my luncheon with him, and then sitting on the turf we talked for an hour about the birds and other wild creatures which he knew best. He told me that he was paid twelve and sixpence a week, and had no prospect of a rise, as the farmers in that part had made a firm stand against the high wages (in some cases amounting to eighteen shillings) which were being paid at other points. I was tempted as an experiment to speak slightingly of the shepherd's homely trade. It was all very well in summer, I said, but what about winter, when the hills were all white with snow; when the wind blew so strong that a man could not walk against or face it; when it was wet all day, and when all nature was drowned in a dense fog, and you cannot see a sheep twenty yards off? "We are accustomed to all weathers, " he replied. "We do not mind the wet and cold—we don't feel it. " I persisted that he earned too little, that shepherding was not good enough for him. He said that his father had been a shepherd all his life, and was now old and becoming infirm; that he (the son) lived in the same cottage, and at odd times helped the old man with his flock, and was able to do a good many little things for him which he could not very well do for himself, and would not be able to pay a stranger to do them. That, I said, was all right and proper; but his father being infirm would not be able to follow a flock many years longer on the hills, and when the old man's shepherding days were over the son would be free. Besides, I added, a young man wants a wife—how could he marry on twelve and sixpence a week? At that there came a pleasant far-away look in his eyes: it could be seen that they were turned inward and were occupied with the image of a particular, incomparable She. He smiled, and appeared to think that it was not impossible to marry on twelve and sixpence a week.

CHAPTER VII

SHEPHERDS AND WHEATEARS

The shepherd's altered condition—His loss of the wheatear harvest—The passion for wheatears—Arrival of the birds on the downs—"Our ortolan"—Coops—The wheatear's habits—Sensitiveness to rain—Hurdis and the "pence of ransom"—A great dame collecting wheatears—JohnDude-ney's recollections—Shepherds cease taking wheatears—Probable reason—How the birds are now obtained—Bird-catchers, poulterers, and farmers—The law must be enforced—Lark-eating.

To all those who love the Sussex Downs and their people it must be a source of regret that the old system of giving the shepherd an interest in the flock was ever changed. According to the old system he was paid a portion of his wages in kind—so many lambs at lambing time; and these, when grown, he was permitted to keep with the flock to the number of twenty or twenty-five, and sometimes perhaps more. At shearing time he was paid for the wool, and he had the increase of his ewes to sell each year. He was thus in a small way in partnership with his master, the farmer, and regarded himself, and was also regarded by others, as something more than a mere hireling, like the shepherd of to-day, who looks to receive a few pieces of silver at each week's end, and will be no better off and no worse off whether the years be fat or lean.

One would imagine that the old system must have worked well on the downs, as it undoubtedly does in other lands where I have known it, and I can only suppose that its discontinuance was the result of that widening of the line dividing employer from employed which has been so general. The farmer did not improve his position by the change—I believe he lost more than he gained: it was simply that the old relations between master and servant were out of date. He was a better educated man, less simple in his life than his forefathers, and therefore at a greater distance from his shepherd; it would remove all friction and simplify things generally to put the shepherd on the same level with the field labourer and other servants: and this was done by giving him a shilling more a week in exchange for the four or five or six lambs he had been accustomed to receive every year.

There have been other, although less important, changes in the life of the lonely man who follows his flock on the hills: one that has a special interest for me refers to the annual wheatear harvest, which was formerly a source of considerable profit to the shepherds of the South Downs. Those who engaged in taking the birds were accustomed to make each season from four or five pounds to twenty—occasionally thirty or forty—pounds. A few shepherds have been known to make as much as fifty pounds. Thus the most successful actually made more by wheatear-catching from July to September than the farmers paid them for the whole year's shepherding. It is sometimes said that wheatears are not now eaten, and that the shepherds no longer take them, because the birds are now so few in number that it would not be worth anyone's while to catch them. There is no doubt that they have decreased very much; but they are still eaten, though the shepherds do not catch them, and, as we shall see presently, the complaint that they have decreased is so old that we read of its having been made a century ago.

The passion for wheatears, so far as I know, was confined to a part of the south coast, and dates some centuries back in time. At all events, it existed and was strong in the time of the Stuarts, and at a later period the demand for the birds increased with the growth of the coast towns of Eastbourne and Brighton.

The pretty little grey and white, black-winged bird that loves the stony desert places of the earth is a strict emigrant, returning to and quitting these shores earlier than most species; and in July, after rearing their young, the southward movement begins, and from all parts of England and Wales, and from Scotland and the islands, the birds come in pairs and in small parties of half a dozen or more to the downs. They are most abundant on the higher part of the range called the South Downs, where they spend a few days on the hills, running and flitting over the close-cropped turf, and playfully pursuing one another in the air. It is a season of rest and recreation on the "threshold of England" before their voyage over sea and subsequent long journey into the interior of a distant continent; and when, having rested, they depart, they are succeeded by others, so that they are never, or but rarely, abundant at any one time, but are always arriving and always departing. They are very fat when they arrive on the downs, and the season during which the shepherds took them, from mid-July to mid-September, must have been a blessed time for the gourmets of the past. Whenever the wheatear ("our ortolan, " as it was affectionately called) is mentioned by writers of two or three centuries ago, the charm of the bird (on the table) is so rapturously dwelt upon, with such an air of rolling a fat delicious morsel in the mouth, and smacking the lips after deglutition, and stroking a well-satisfied stomach, that one is led to think that the happiness of the great, the wise, and the good of that age was centred in their bellies, and that they looked on the eating of wheatears as the highest pleasure man could know; unless indeed they considered it an even higher one "to see all their friends drunk and happy about them. "

In July the shepherds made their "coops, " as their traps were called—a T-shaped trench about fourteen inches long, over which the two long narrow sods cut neatly out of the turf were adjusted, grass downwards. A small opening was left at the end for ingress, and there was room in the passage for the bird to pass through toward the chinks of light coming from the two ends of the cross passage. At the inner end of the passage a horse-hair springe was set, by which the bird was caught by the neck as it passed in, but the noose did not as a rule strangle the bird.

On some of the high downs near the coast, notably at Beachy Head, at Birling Gap, at Seaford, and in the neighbourhood of Rottingdean, the shepherds made so many coops, placed at small distances apart, that the downs in some places looked as if they had been ploughed. In September, when the season was over, the sods were carefully put back, roots down, in their places, and the smooth green surface was restored to the hills.

The wheatear when travelling flies low, and has the habit of alighting on any barren or stony piece of ground. If a heap of flints be collected, or a few sods be turned earth upwards, not a bird will come in sight of the place but will go out of his way to settle on it, and the larger the patch of ground thrown into coops the more birds come to it. Again, the bird has the habit of going into any hole or crevice it finds in the stony or barren spots it loves to visit. I have noticed the same habit in birds of other species that breed in dark holes. The fact that on bright and cloudless days few wheatears were caught in the coops and that considerable numbers were always taken on days of flying clouds and of shadow and sunlight, seems to show that the birds make use of the holes as a shelter. They probably greatly dislike being wetted by rain; and indeed the bird's safety must in a great degree depend on his ability to keep himself dry, since a wet plumage interferes with flight, and the wheatear, on account of his conspicuous plumage, as well as of the open exposed character of the ground he inhabits, must be more liable than almost any other species to be attacked by hawks that prey upon small birds. The sudden gloom caused by a cloud obscuring the sun is the forerunner of a swift-coming storm to the bird, a sudden shadow being associated with rain in his mind, and he flies to shelter himself in the nearest hole; and if the gloom falls on the earth fifty or a hundred times a day he will act in the same way every time. It was owing to this extreme sensitiveness of the wheatear, and its inability to distinguish between a rain-cloud and a cloud without rain, that the shepherds were so successful in taking them in their simple traps. So well did the shepherd know this habit and weakness of the bird, that on a dry day of unbroken cloud he did not look to get more than a few birds; on a day of continual sunshine he hardly thought it worth while to visit his coops; but on a day of flying clouds and broken lights he would go the round of his coops three or four times to collect the birds and reset the snares.

Hurdis, the poet of the downs, in *The Favorite Village*, in a long passage on the subject of wheatear-catching, has the following lines:

So when the fevered cloud of August day
Flits through the blue expanse...
The timorous wheatear, fearful of the shade,
Trips to the hostile shelter of the clod,
And where she sought protection finds a snare.

... Seized by the springe
She flutters for lost liberty in vain,
A costly morsel, destined for the board
Of well-fed luxury, if no kind friend,
No gentle passenger the noose dissolve,
And give her to her free-born wing again.
Incautious bird, such as thy lot is now,
Such once was mine...

And in the end, recalling how he was delivered and by whom, he resolves that his hand shall "at distance imitate" —-

And to the feathery captive give release.
The pence of ransom placing in its stead.
Go, fool, be cheated of thy wing no more!

His "pence of ransom" requires a word of explanation. It was customary for those who required a supply of wheatears for a big dinner, when there were none or not enough to be had in the market, to go out themselves to the downs and collect them from the coops, and to leave the price of as many birds as were found caught and taken. All the coops from which the birds were taken were left uncovered, and a small pile of silver and copper coins, the market value of the birds, placed in the last trench. The shepherd going the rounds of his coops would count the money, reset the springes, and go back satisfied to his flock.

When the tender-hearted clergyman-poet left his pence for the birds, which he took from the coops merely to set them free, his neighbours must have regarded him as an exceedingly eccentric person, for the birds were caught to be eaten by important persons in Sussex; indeed, the wheatear was created for that purpose, even as the robin redbreast, wren, and swallow—sacred birds in other lands—were made to be eaten by the people of Italy.

A middle-aged man, a native of the village of East Dean, described to me how a very great lady of Eastbourne, who entertained a good deal, and liked her birds fresh caught, used often to go out driving in a carriage and pair on the downs; and he, a boy of twelve, used to run after the carriage in hopes of getting a penny; and how, on arriving at a number of coops, the big liveried footman would jump down and uncover coop after coop and wring the necks of the little birds he took out, until he had got as many as his mistress wanted, and then she would hand him the money to leave in a trench, and the carriage would drive off.

A shepherd of the South Downs, named John Dudeney, afterwards a schoolmaster in Lewes, where I believe one or two of his granddaughters still keep a school, was included by M. A. Lower in his *Worthies of Sussex*, on account of his passion for books and other virtues. And it will be allowed by everyone that a poor peasant youth, who, when shepherding on the hills, acquired a knowledge of astronomy and of other out-of-the-way subjects, and taught himself to read the Bible in Hebrew, was deserving of a place among the lesser celebrities of his county.

In a too-short account which Dudeney gave of his early life and struggles to make money enough to buy books as well as to live, there is an interesting note or two on his experiences as a wheatear-catcher. Here is a picture of his early shepherding days:

I have sometimes been on the hills in winter from morning to night, and have not seen a single person during the whole day. In the snow I have walked to and fro under the shelter of a steep bank, or in a bottom or a combe, while my sheep have been by me scraping away the snow with their forefeet to get at the grass, and I have taken my book out of my pocket, and as I walked to and fro in the snow have read to pass away the time. It is very cold on the downs in such weather. I remember once, whilst with my father, the snow froze into ice on my eyelashes, and he breathed on my face to thaw it off. The downs are very pleasant in summer.

Yes, they are.

At midsummer, 1799, I removed to Kingston, near Lewes, where I was under-shepherd for three years. The flock was large (1400), and my master, the head shepherd, being old and infirm, much of the labour devolved on me. While here I had better wages, 6 pounds a year; I had also part of the money obtained from the sale of wheatears, though we did not catch them here in great numbers, a dozen or two a day, seldom more. The hawks often injured us by tearing them out of their coops, scattering their feathers about, which frightened the other birds from the coops. During winter I caught the moles, which, at twopence each, brought me a few shillings.

It is a pity that Dudeney did not give the name of the bold hawk that tore the captive birds out of the coops. The kite, buzzard, harriers, as well as peregrine falcon and sparrow-hawk, were common in those days. Some of the old shepherds say that the stoats were a great nuisance, and robbed them of a good many birds. One old shepherd, who caught wheatears for many years near Seaford, told me that the starlings gave him most trouble. They would go poking into the coops and get themselves caught. They were unsaleable, and so he ate them. As soon as he took them out of the traps he pulled their heads off. That, he informed me, is the only proper thing to do. If you pull off their heads they are good to eat, but if you leave their heads on they are not good.

I always leave my starlings' heads on.

Dudeney next tells us what he did at Westside Farm, at Rottingdean, where he was afterwards engaged.

The farm extending along the sea-coast, I caught great numbers of wheatears during the season for taking them, which lasted from the middle of July to the end of August. The most I ever caught in one day was thirteen dozen. We sold them to a poulterer at Brighton, who took all we could catch at eighteenpence a dozen. From what I have heard from old shepherds, it cannot be doubted that they were caught in much greater numbers a century ago than of late. I have heard them speak of an immense number being taken in one day by a shepherd of East Dean, near Beachy Head. I think they said he took nearly a hundred dozen; so many that he could not thread them on crow-quills in the usual manner, but took off his round frock and made a sack of it to pop them into, and his wife did the same with her petticoat. This must have been when there was a great flight. Their numbers are now so decreased that some shepherds do not set up any coops, as it does not pay for the trouble.

This last statement describing the state of things a century ago struck me as very curious when I first read it; that the birds had now decreased so much that it was not worth while setting up coops, was precisely what the shepherds had said when I asked them why they had given up catching the wheatears. But it is not the truth, or not the whole truth. For about eighty years after Dudeney's days at Rottingdean, the shepherds in that neighbourhood and all along the South Down range continued to catch wheatears, and were glad to do so. There is one old firm of poulterers in Brighton whose custom it was to pay the shepherds for all the birds they sent in at the end of the season. When pay-day arrived the shepherds would come in, and a very substantial dinner with plenty of beer would be served to them; and after the meal and toasts and songs every man would be paid his money. At these yearly dinners, which were continued down to about 1880, as many as fifty shepherds have been known to attend. Yet this firm could not have had more than a third or a fourth part of the wheatears supplied by the shepherds to deal with.

About the date just named, or a little later, the Rottingdean farmers began to forbid their shepherds engaging to supply the Brighton poulterers with wheatears: the men, they said, were so much occupied in going the rounds of their coops that they neglected their proper work. The example of these farmers spread over the downs, and their action was, so far as I know, the real cause of the somewhat sudden abandonment by the shepherds of their ancient supplementary trade of catching wheatears. That they no longer follow it is a cause of profound regret to the poulterers, for the demand still exists and must somehow be supplied. Fowlers were engaged to go out and shoot and trap the birds the best way they could, but the shot so injured the delicate plump little bodies that this method was discontinued. For some years past the big poulterers have been compelled to engage the services of the ordinary bird-catcher of the Brighton slums, who takes the birds with the common clapnets. His method is to go out with a couple of "pals" to help and to spread his nests at the side of one of the small solitary dew-ponds on the hills. In very dry hot weather there are always some wheatears flitting and running about on the turf in the neighbourhood of the pond, to which they go at intervals to drink. The nets spread, the helpers make a wide circuit, and when they see a few birds walk quietly towards them, making them move on towards the pond. Once they are near it and spy one of their kind (the decoy wheatear tied to a peg) they fly to it and are taken in the nets. The number of birds taken in this slow laborious way is not enough to meet the demand that still exists. "We could, " said one of the largest men in the trade at Brighton to me last summer, "sell four times as many wheatears as we can get at six shilling a dozen. "

It is curious to have to add that the industrious bird-catcher cannot now get even this insufficient supply of birds without exposing himself to the risk of prosecutions and fines.

In the East Sussex bird-protection order, which was made law in June 1897, the wheatear is a scheduled bird, and is therefore fully protected during the close time, which, in that county, extends to September I. The wheatears are in season and are taken in July and August. The poulterers and game-dealers in the coast towns, and some of the farmers, are in league with the bird-catcher, and are perhaps more deserving of punishment than the man from the slums who does the dirty work. A certain number of farmers, who do not mind what they do if they are paid, allow bird-catchers to have a "pitch" on their land, and are not ashamed to take some small sum, usually ten to twenty shillings a year, for the privilege. The bird-catcher spreads his nets as far from the road as he can, and gives out that he is catching starlings with the farmer's permission. The starling is not a scheduled bird, and, though protected, may be taken by any person on his own land, or by anyone with the owner's consent. Catching wheatears for starlings has gone on unpunished until now, or rather to the end of the last close time in East Sussex, September 1, 1899, and ought not to be any longer tolerated. When the wheatear season comes round once more efforts will, I trust, be made by residents on the south coast, who are anxious to preserve our wild bird life, to enforce the law; and I hope to be there to help them.

It is often said that the wheatears have decreased, and will continue to decrease, owing to the continual spread of cultivation and the consequent diminution of the open, barren, and stony lands which the bird inhabits. All the more need then to put an end to the wholesale taking of the birds when they arrive on the South Downs, during migration. The wheatear is a pretty, interesting bird, a sweet singer, and dear to all who love the wildness and solitude of hills and of desert, stony places. It is not fair that it should be killed merely to enable London stockbrokers, sporting men, and other gorgeous persons who visit the coast, accompanied by ladies with yellow hair, to feed every day on "ortolans" at the big Brighton hotels.

Lark-eating, which revolts us even more than wheatear-eating, is, alas! too common and widespread in the country to be suppressed in the same easy way. It will not soon be ended—there are too many Britons with the Italian's debased passion for a song-bird's flesh. But the feeling of intense disgust and even abhorrence the practice arouses in all lovers of nature grows, and will continue to grow; and we may look forward to the time when the feeders on skylarks of to-day will be dead and themselves eaten by worms, and will have no successors in all these islands.

CHAPTER VIII

SILENCE AND MUSIC

The art of music—Natural music—Sussex voices—A pretty girl with a musical voice—Singing of the peasants—Dr. Burton on Sussex singing—Primitive singing—A shepherdess and her cries—The Sussex sheep-dog's temper—Silence of the hills—Bird music of the downs—Common bunting—Linnet—Stonechat—Whinchat—The distance which sound travels—Experience with tramps—Singing of skylarks—Effects which cannot be expressed.

Perhaps it would be as well to explain at the outset that about music proper I have next to nothing to say in spite of the heading of this chapter. Music is inexpressibly delightful, but when I am with or very near to or fresh from nature 1 am cold to it; and when listening I am in a curious way more than fastidious. That which is wholly satisfying to the trained followers and professors, who live and move and have their beings in a perpetual concord of sweet sounds; that which they regard as perfection and the best expression of all that is best in man, is not a great thing to me. Even when it most enchants me, if it does not wholly swamp my intellect, I have a sense of something abnormal in it, or at all events, of something wholly out of proportion to and out of harmony with things as they exist. That music comes to us naturally, that it is an instinct, nobody will deny; it is only music as an art and an end in itself, cultivated in the highest degree for its own sake alone, and taken out of its relation with life, that I am compelled to regard as a mere by-product of the mind, a beautiful excrescence, which is of no importance to the race, and without which most of us are just as rich and happy in our lives.

This question does not concern us. Music in another wider sense is, like beauty, everywhere—the elemental music of winds and of waters, of

The lisp of leaves and the ripple of rain,

and the music of bird voices. For just as the bird, as Ruskin says, is the cloud concentrated, its aerial form perfected and vivified with life; so, too, in the songs and calls and cries of the winged people do we listen to the diffused elemental music of nature concentrated and changed to clear penetrative sound. Listen to the concealed reed-warbler, quietly singing all day long to himself among the reeds and rushes: it is a series of liquid sounds, the gurgling and chiming of lapping water on the shallow pebbled bed of a stream. The beautiful inflected cry of the playing pewit is a mysterious lonely sound, as of some wild half-human being blowing in a hollow reed he had made. Listen again to a band of small shore birds—stints, dotterels, knots, and dunlins—conversing together as they run about on the level sands, or dropping bright twittering notes as they fly swiftly past: it is like the vibrating crystal chiming sounds of a handful of pebbles thrown upon and bounding and glissading musically over a wide sheet of ice.

From these small sounds and the smaller still of insect life, to the greater sounds of bird and mammal—the noise of the herring and black-backed gulls drifting leisurely by at a vast height above the earth, and ever and anon bursting out in a great chorus of laugh-like cries, as if the clouds had laughed; the innumerable tremulous bleatings of a driven flock; the percussive bark of the shepherd's dog, and the lowing of kine in some far-off valley. They are all musical, and are in a sense music. And, best of all, there is the human voice. Even a musical artist, in spite of an artist's prejudice, an old English composer, has said that speech, the sweet music of it, is infinitely more to us than song and the sound of all our musical instruments.

I cannot say that the Sussexians have more musical voices than the people of any other part of the kingdom, but their speech is pleasant, more so than in most counties, and they are certainly fond of singing. The people of the downs have in my experience the nicest voices in speaking. And here as in other places you will occasionally find a voice of the purest, most beautiful quality. I would go more miles to hear a voice of that description speaking simple words, than I would go yards to listen to the most wonderful vocal flights of the greatest diva on earth. Not that the mere pleasure to the sense would not be vastly greater in the latter case; but in the other the voice, though but of a peasant saying some simple thing, would also say something to the mind, and would live and re-live in the mind, to be heard again and often, even after years; and with other similar voices it would serve to nourish and keep alive a dream. And after all a dream may be a man's best possession; though it be but of an immeasurably remote future—a time when these tentative growths, called art, and valued as the highest good attainable —the bright consummate flower of intellect—shall have withered, and, like tendrils no longer needed, dropped forgotten from the human plant.

One such voice I heard to my great delight in or near a hamlet not many miles from Singleton in the West Sussex Downs. Sauntering along the path in a quiet green very pretty place, I spied a girl pushing a perambulator with a baby in it before her, using one hand, while in the other hand she held an apple, which she was just beginning to eat. It was a very big apple, all of the purest apple-green colour except where she had bitten into it, and there it was snowy white. She was a slim, gracefully-formed girl of about fifteen, with the Sussex round face and fine features, but with a different colour, for her skin was a clear dark one, her eyes soft deep blue, and her unbound hair, which was very abundant and very fine, was black, but showing chestnut-brown where the wind had fluffed it about her face. Perhaps her mouth, with its delicately-moulded lips, was her finest feature; and it was very pretty, as she came up to where I stood waiting for her, to see her small, even, sharp, pearly teeth cut into the polished green apple. But though she was so lovely to look at, if I had allowed her to pass by without speaking the probability is that her image would have soon faded out of memory. We see and straightway forget many a pretty face. But when I spoke to her and she answered in a musical voice of so beautiful a quality, that was like a blackbird's voice and a willow-wren's, yet better than either, the rare sweet sound registered itself in my brain, and with it the face, too, became unforgettable. When she had given me her answer I thought of other things to ask—the name of the next village (which I knew) and the next, and the distance to each, with many other unnecessary inquiries, and still every time she spoke it was more to me than a "melody sweetly played in tune"; and it was at last with the greatest reluctance that I was compelled to thank her and let her go.

As to the singing of the Sussex peasants, I must confess that it has amused rather than delighted me, but at the same time it is interesting. You can best hear it in the village ale-house or inn in the evening, especially on a Saturday, when a pleasant break in the week has come with rest from toil, and money has been paid for wages, and life has a more smiling aspect than on most days. Beer, too, of which unusually large quantities are consumed at such times, makes glad the Sussexian heart, and song is with him the natural expression of the feeling. Willum, asked for a song, without much demur sings it with all his heart; he is followed by Tummas, who scarcely waits to be asked; and then Gaarge, who began clearing his throat and moistening his lips when Tummas was in the fourteenth and last stanza, bursts out with his rollicking song with a chorus in which all join. Then follow Sammel and Bill (to distinguish him from Willum), and finally John Birkenshaw, the silent man, who has been occupied all the evening drinking beer and saying nothing, gives by general request his celebrated murder ballad in twenty-three stanzas. Before it is quite finished, when he is pointing the moral of his gruesome tale, warning all fond mothers to look well after their daughters dear, and not foolishly allow them to go out walking with young men of doubtful reputation, the listeners begin to yawn and look drowsy; but they praise his performance when it is happily over, and John wipes his forehead, drinks his beer, and says good-night.

As to their manner of singing, it was admirably described about the middle of the eighteenth century by a Dr. John Burton, a clergyman, who was accustomed to "travel" into Sussex at intervals, and who recorded his observations on the country and its people in an amusing work entitled *Iter Sussexiense*.

It has been remarked of the modern writer, Jules Janin, that when all the good work he has produced has been forgotten by the world, he will still be remembered by his unconsciously humorous description of the lobster as "the Cardinal of the Sea. " A fate of that kind has befallen Burton, who is remembered only as the author of an exceedingly ridiculous saying. He affirms that oxen, pigs, and women are long-legged in this county, and, speculating as to the reason, asks: "May it be from the difficulty of pulling the feet out of so much mud by the strength of the ankle that the muscles get stretched, as it were, and the bones lengthened? "

Of the Sussex manner of speaking and singing, Dr. Burton wrote:

They raise their voices to a sharp pitch, and moreover deliver all their words fluently and in a sort of sing-song.... The more shrill-toned they may be, the more valued they are; and in church they sing psalms by preference, not set to the old simple tune, but as if in tragic chorus, changing about with strophe and antistrophe and stanza, with good measure, but yet there is something offensive to my ears, when they bellow to excess and bleat out some goatish noise with all their might.

The description is true of to-day, only the goatish noise, which is offensive to most ears, is not now heard so much in church, where indeed the Sussex peasant is not often seen: you hear it in the alehouse and the cottage.

What strikes me as the most curious and interesting point about their singing—their love of high-pitched voices, and, in many of their ballads, their go-as-you-please tuneless tuneful manner, with the prolonging of some notes at random and "bleating out of goatish noises"—is its resemblance to the singing of the Basques, which is perhaps the most primitive kind of vocal music that survives in Europe. This Basque singing in its turn strongly reminds me of all the Indians' singing I have heard in South America, including that of the Tehuelches—the Patagonian nomad race. The gauchos of the pampas, too, have inherited something of that manner of singing from their progenitors, or else have caught it from the aborigines. The Basques and the red men, like our Sussexians, are fond of shrillness and acute sounds, but do not, like the East Indians, cultivate falsetto.

I have described the sweetest, most musical voice heard in Sussex as that of a young girl in the downs; another downland girl's voice was one of the acutest carrying voices I ever heard in my life. She was shepherding (a rare thing for a girl to do) on the very high downs between Stanmer and Westmeston; and for two or three days during my rambles among the hills in that neighbourhood I constantly heard her oft-repeated calls and long piercing cries sounding wonderfully loud and distinct even at a distance of two miles and more away. It was like the shrill echoing cries of some clear-voiced big bird—some great forest fowl, or eagle, or giant ibis, or rail, or courlan, in some far land where great birds with glorious voices have not all been extirpated.

It was nice to hear, but it surprised me that all that outcry, heard over an area of seven or eight square miles, was necessary. At a distance of a mile I watched her, and saw that she had no dog, that her flock, numbering nine hundred, travelled a good deal, being much distressed by thirst, as all the dew-ponds in that part of the downs were dry. When her far-sounding cries failed to make them turn then she had to go after them, and her activity and fleetness of foot were not less remarkable than her ringing voice; but I pitied her doing a man and dog's work in that burning weather, and towards evening on my way home I paid her a visit. She was a rather lean but wiry-looking girl, just over fifteen years old, with an eager animated face, dark skin and blackish fuzzy hair and dark eyes. She was glad to talk and explain it all, and had a high-pitched but singularly agreeable voice and spoke rapidly and well. The shepherd had been called away, and no shepherd boy could be found to take his place: all the men were harvesting, and the flock had been given into her charge. The shepherd had left his dog, but he would not obey her: she had taken him out several days, leading him by a cord, but no sooner would she release him than he would run home, and so she had given up trying.

I advised her to try again, and the next day I spent some time watching her, the dog at her side, calling and crying her loudest, flying over the wide hill-side after the sheep; but the dog cared not where they went, and sullenly refused to obey her. Here is a dog, thought I, with good, old-fashioned, conservative ideas about the employment of women: he is not going to help them make themselves shepherdesses on the South Downs. A probably truer explanation of the animal's rebellious behaviour was given by a young shepherd of my acquaintance. The dog, he said, refused to do what he was told because the girl was not his master's daughter, nor of his house. The sheep-dog's attachment to the family is always very strong, and he will gladly work for any member of it; but for no person outside. "My dog, " he added, "will work as willingly and as well for any one of my sisters, when I leave the flock to their care, as he will for me; but he would not stir a foot for any person, man or woman, not of the family. " He said, too, that this was the common temper of the Sussex sheep-dog; faithful above all dogs to their own people but suspicious of all strangers, and likely at any time to bite the stranger's hand that caresses them.

I daresay he was right: I have made the acquaintance of some scores of these downland dogs, and greatly admired them, especially their brown eyes, which are more eloquent and human in their expression than any other dog's eyes known to me; yet it has frequently happened that after I had established, as I imagined, a firm friendship with one, he has suddenly snapped or growled at me.

My account of that most extraordinary hullaballoo among the hills made by the young shepherdess has served to remind me of the subject I had set myself to write about in this chapter, and which in all these pages I have not yet touched upon—the wonderful silence of the downs, and the effect of nature's more delicate music heard in such an atmosphere. That clear repeated call of the young shepherdess would have sounded quite different from six to eight hundred feet below on the flat weald, where it would have mixed with other sounds, and a denser atmosphere and hedges and trees would have muffled and made it seem tame and commonplace. On the great smooth hills, because of their silence and their thinner, purer atmosphere, it fell startlingly on the sense, and the prolonged cries had a wild and lonely expression.

This silence of the hills does not impress one at once if the mind is occupied with thinking, or the eyes with seeing. But if one spends many hours each day and many days in lonely rambles (and who would not prefer to be alone in such a place?) a consciousness of it grows upon the mind. The quiet, too, becomes increasingly grateful, and the contrast between the hills and the lowland grows sharper with each day. Coming down to the village where one sleeps, it seems like a town full of business and noise, and the sound of a train in the distance has a strangely disturbing effect. The coarse and common sounds of the lowlands do not penetrate into the silent country of the hills. The sounds there are mostly of birds, and these are comparatively few and are not the loud-voiced. Furthermore, when they are the same voices which you are accustomed to hear in hedge and field and orchard, they do not seem quite the same. The familiar note of the homestead has a more delicate, spiritualised sound. The common characteristic songsters of the islands and miniature forests of furze are the linnet, white-throat, dunnock, meadow pipit, yellowhammer, common bunting, whinchat, and stonechat. They are none of them loud-voiced, and their songs do not drown or kill one another, but are rather in harmony and suited to that bright quiet land. I have said that the song—thrush among other birds of the orchard goes to the downs and sometimes breeds there. Now, although I am as fond of the music of this thrush as anyone can be, heard from the tree-tops in woods and lanes and fields, where it sounds best, it was never a welcome voice on the downs. I seldom heard it in those wilder quiet furze islands among the high hills; and if the loud staccato song burst out in such a place I always had a strong inclination to go out of my way and throw a stone at the singer to silence him. On the other hand, I never tired of listening to even the poorest of the characteristic species; even the common bunting was a constant pleasure. In the wide sunny world I preferred him to his neighbour and relation, the yellowhammer. The sound he emits by way of song is certainly bright, and, like some other bird-voices, it is associated in my mind in hot and brilliant weather with the appearance of water spouting or leaping and sparkling in the sun. Doubtless such expressions as "needles of sound, " "splinters, " and "shafts, " and "jets of sound, " etc., to be found in writers on bird-music, are not wholly metaphorical, but actually express the connection existing in the writer's mind between certain sounds and sights. The common bunting's little outburst of confused or splintered notes, is when heard (by me) at the same time mentally seen as a handful of clear water thrown up and breaking into sparkling drops in the sunlight. Of the songsters of the furze on the downs the best to my mind is the stonechat. It is true that the linnet has one exquisite note, the equal of which for purest melody and tender expression is not to be found among our feathered vocalists. Those who are so utterly without imagination as to keep a linnet (for the love of it) in a wire prison, cannot hear this note as I hear it. To sing it properly the little bird must be free of the summer sunshine, the wide blue sky and green expanse of earth, the furze bushes, aflame with their winged blossoms and smelling of spice; for that incomparable note, and the carmine colour which comes not on his feathers in captivity, express his gladness in a free aerial life.

If we except that one angelical note, the linnet is nearly on a level as a singer with the other species I have named; but the stonechat comes first in the order of merit, and I think the whinchat comes next. The ornithological books on this point tell us only that the stonechat has a short and simple, or a short but pleasant (or not unpleasant) song; and there is indeed not much more to say of it as we usually hear it. No sooner does he catch sight of a human form in his haunts than he is all excitement and trouble, and will flit and perch and flit again from bush-top to bush-top, perpetual uttering his two little contrasted alarm-notes, the *chack, chack,* as of two pebbles struck together, which he has in common with other chats, and the thin little sorrowful piping sound. This anxious temper keeps him from singing in our presence, and causes us to think that he sings but rarely. Then, too, his voice is not strong, and does not carry well, and it is not strange that when heard in a place where bird-notes are many and loud it attracts but little attention. Heard in the perfect silence of the downland atmosphere, where the slightest sound flies far, it strikes me as a very delicate and beautiful song, in its character unlike that of any other British species.

One day last June I had a pleasant experience with this bird. I sat still among bushes, where stone-chats were breeding, until they got over their anxiety or forgot my presence, and began to sing; first one and then another, and at last I had three singing within hearing distance. To sing the stonechat flies up almost vertically from his perch on the topmost spray of a bush to a height of forty or fifty to a hundred feet, and at the highest point pours out a rapid series of double notes, the first clear and sharp, the next deeper or somewhat throaty, then the clear again, the und rising and falling rhythmically; and as he sin. ne drops rapidly a distance of a couple of feet, then flutters up and drops again and again. It is both dance and song, and a very pretty performance.

The whinchat's song is even less well known, or less regarded, than that of its more conspicuously coloured relation, the stonechat. Thus, William Borrer, in his *Birds of Sussex*, expresses the opinion that this species has no song; yet he had spent eighty years of his long life in a rural district where the whinchat is fairly common, and had been a lifelong observer of the birds of his county. It is in fact a low gentle song that cannot be heard far, and when other birds are singing it is not regarded. The song is a warble of half a dozen notes, and is hardly longer than the redstart's song, with which it has been compared. But it is not like it. The whinchat's best notes, though low, have a full, sweet, mellow quality which makes them comparable to the blackbird and the blackcap. The redstart's best and opening note is bright, yet plaintive, and reminds one at the same time of two such unlike songsters as the swallow and the robin.

Sitting quietly on a low bush the whinchat will sometimes warble for half an hour at a stretch, uttering his few notes, and repeating them after an interval so short as to produce at a little distance the effect of a continuous warble like that of the garden-warbler or sedge-warbler. But he is never like them, excited, and in a hurry to get his notes out: he sings in a leisurely manner. Now one June day in a furzy place I began to hear the almost continuous warble of the bird, and standing still I tried to catch sight of him in a clump about fifty yards away. I was sure he was in that clump and could not be further away, for even a distance of fifty yards was almost too far to hear so low a song distinctly. I sat down to listen and watch, and the song, very sweet and beautiful, went on and on, and still I could see nothing. At length I got up and went to the clump and saw no bird, but the song still went on no louder than before: I walked, following up the sound, and discovered the bird at a distance of over four hundred yards from where I had began to listen to it.

I was greatly surprised on this occasion at the distance sound will travel on these silent hills; I was still more surprised on another day when I met with an amusing experience.

Sometimes, when in some very lonely spot, such as I loved to spend a day in, human voices were distinctly heard coming from a great distance when no human form was in sight. I was reminded of poor Peter Wilkins, alone in his desolate antarctic island, listening during the long polar night to the mysterious sounds of invisible people talking and laughing, now on this side, now on that, or else far up in the pale dim sky. But these voices did not make me miserable; I had my "beautiful creatures" for company, and wished not for other. Still I did not wholly escape from my own kind. One afternoon in July, in the loneliest spot I knew, where half the side of a great down is overgrown with luxuriant furze, I heard a sound of eager talking, as of persons engaged in argument, which appeared to grow louder and louder; and at last I spied coming down into the wilderness of furze three human figures, and turning my binocular on them made out that they were three very unpleasant-looking tramps, each with a big bundle, and they were evidently coming to camp at that place. After I had been observing them for some time they all at once caught sight of me, standing motionless among the bushes at a distance of about six hundred yards, and were thrown into a great state of excitement. "Don't lose sight of him! Keep your eye on him while I hide the things away! " I heard one cry to the others, after which he disappeared for some time among the bushes. For half an hour longer they kept their eyes on me, and at length the one who had hidden his treasures away, plucking up courage, came towards me, and when within about fifty yards began to explain that he and his mates were doing no harm, but had only come to that spot to cook a bit of food and to rest. I answered that I didn't mind — what they did there was no business of mine. That greatly relieved him; for having guilty consciences, they doubtless had jumped to the conclusion that I was there in the interests of the landlord to attend to the safety of the rabbits and warn off suspicious-looking human beings. He then took notice of my curiously-shaped binocular, and asked me what I used it for. I told him that it was for watching birds — that was my business, and I would attend to it and leave him to attend to his. I spoke a little sharply, not because of any feeling of enmity towards tramps generally, but because he was a singularly unpleasant specimen. He was a small man with low cunning and rascality written on his dirty face, in ancient corduroys, waistcoat all rags, and a once black frock coat, too big for him, shining with dirt and grease as if it had been japanned in patches: a rusty bowler hat and broken earth-coloured boots completed his attire. His manner was even worse—or rather both of his manners, for at first he had cringed and was now jaunty. He took the hint and went back to his companions.

Three days later I spent the last half of a day at the same place. There was a stony spot there, where the ground was quite covered with bleached flints, with many chipped specimens among them, and late in the day, while waiting for the sun to set, I amused myself by turning over and examining these fragments. A babble of voices in eager discussion reached my ears and grew louder and nearer, and at length I spied coming over the hill towards me the same three vagabonds I had met there before. And again, on first catching sight of me stooping among the bushes, they were greatly alarmed, and becoming silent separated and hid themselves in the furze. After watching me for some time they made the discovery that I was the harmless person whose business it was to watch birds encountered some days before, and coming out from hiding they went on their way. When they had got past me the same man who had talked with me on the former occasion turned back and came up to where I was standing. He still wanted to talk, but I did not encourage him. Then he stood silent for some time watching me picking up flints, and at last he said, "I see that you are interested in flints. I found a very curious one the other day, which I think you would like to see. It is perfectly round like a bullet, and weighs about a pound. It has a hole in it, and I think it is hollow inside. I hid it under a furze bush, and you can see it if you will go to the place with me. " I told him that perfectly round flints with a hollow inside were quite common on the downs: that if I wanted any I could find a dozen, or twenty, or forty any day. It surprised him, he said, to hear that round flints were so common, as he had never seen but that one. Then he tried to introduce other topics, and, snubbed again, he at last left me and went after his companions. Meanwhile they had been steadily walking on, and when he at last overtook them they were a quarter of a mile from me. On catching them up he exclaimed "I say! " to call attention to something he wished to tell them, and I listened. "The other day, " he said, "that man was a naturalist; to-day he is a geologist! "

It surprised me to hear him use such words, and show so perfect a knowledge of their right meaning; but it amazed me that I had been able to hear them distinctly at that great distance. It was a new experience, and produced a feeling that I had somehow, without noticing it at the time, been re-made and endowed with a new set of senses infinitely better than the old ones. The tramps, unaccustomed to the hills, of course had no idea of the distance their voices carried, or they would not have talked about keeping their eyes on me and hiding their parcels, etc., when they first saw me. I noticed subsequently that lowland people generally spoke a great deal louder than was necessary on the downs. They were accustomed to a denser and noisier atmosphere, and were like people who have been conversing with a deaf person, and when they speak to others cannot drop the habit of shouting. The shepherd's manner of speaking, and his voice too, I think, have been modified somewhat by his surroundings. At all events, he speaks quietly and has a very clear voice; a man with a loud thick speech is not a native of the hills.

But it is when listening to the music of the larks that we are best able to appreciate the wonderful silence of the hills, and the refining effect of long distances in this pure thin atmosphere on the acutest and brightest bird sounds.

The skylark is found all over downland, and is abundant wherever there is cultivation. On the sheep-walks, where favourable breeding-places are comparatively few, he is so thinly distributed that you may sometimes ramble about for half a day and not put up more than half a dozen birds. And yet here, on these sheep-fed hills, out of sight of corn-fields, you hear the lark all day long—not one nor half a dozen, nor a score or two, but many scores, and I should say hundreds of larks. Go where you like, to the summit of the highest hill, or down the longest slopes into the deepest combe or valley at its foot, everywhere you are ringed about with that perpetual unchanging stream of sound. It is not a confused, nor a diffused, sound, which is everywhere, filling the whole air like a misty rain, or a perfume, or like the universal hum of a teeming insect life in a wood in summer; but a sound that ever comes from a great distance, out of the sky: and you are always in the centre of it; and the effect is as of an innumerable company of invisible beings, forming an unbroken circle as wide as the horizon, chanting an everlasting melody in one shrill, unchanging tone. You may hear it continuously for hours, yet look in vain to see a bird; I have strained my sight, gazing for an hour, and have not seen one rising or coming back to earth, and have looked up and listened in vain to hear one singing overhead. And I have looked all about the sky with my strong glasses without being able to detect one small brown speck on the vast blue expanse. This was because the birds on these smooth, close-cropped hills, especially in the dry months of July and August, were really very few and far between—so far, indeed, that not a bird came within ken. And yet on account of the immense distance the sound travels you can hear the voices of hundreds.

The highest notes of the lark on these hills may, I believe, be heard three miles away. That sound carries three times as far on these heights as it does on the level country I am positive; and if this be so, the highest notes of all the birds singing on a windless day within a circuit of eighteen miles are audible. Many, probably most, of the birds one hears are singing over distant corn-fields; but the fields are too far to be seen, or they are on slopes behind interposing summits and ridges. It may happen (it has been my experience many scores of times) that no bird is near enough for the listener to hear any of its lower, harsh, or guttural notes. But if the listener is near a corn-field, or if any birds are singing near him, these guttural notes will be audible, and the effect of the music will not be quite the same.

The song of the lark is a continuous torrent of contrasted guttural and clear shrill sounds and trills, so rapidly emitted that the notes, so different in character, yet seem to interpenetrate or to overlap each other; and the effect on the ear is similar to that on the eye of sober or dull and brilliant colours mixed and running into one another in a confused pattern. The acutest note of all, a clear piercing sound like a cry several times repeated, is like a chance patch of most brilliant colour occurring at intervals in the pattern. As the distance between listener and bird increases the throat-notes cease to be audible; beginning with the lowest they are one by one sifted out, and are followed by the trills; and finally, at a very great distance—as far, in fact, as anything of the song is left—the occasional shrill reiterated notes I have described alone can be heard.

Let the reader, then, who has not been on these downs in summer on a brightest, windless day, and listened alone to this sound—alone, since a companion's talk or even his silent presence would in most cases mar the effect—let him imagine if he can the effect of a great number of birds all round the sky pouring out their highest, shrillest notes, so clarified and brightened by distance as to seem like no earthly music. To say of a sound that it is bright is to use a too common metaphor; this sound shines above all others, and the multitude of voices made one by distance is an effulgence and a glory. I have listened to it by the hour, never wearying nor ceasing to wonder at that mysterious beautiful music which could not be called crystalline nor silvery, but was like the heavenly sunshine translated into sound; subtle, insistent, filling the world and the soul, yet always at a vast distance, falling, falling like a lucid rain. No other sound would have seemed worth listening to there. The richest, most passionate strains of the nightingale, if such a bird had by chance sung near me in a bush, would have seemed no more than the chirruping and chiding of a sparrow. And when I have called to mind the best things our poets have said of the lark, their words have sounded to me strangely commonplace and even insipid: "Up with me, up with me into the clouds"—it is but the common brown bird of the corn-fields, the bird of earth with a nest and a sitting mate, and a song full of harsh guttural sounds mixed with clear notes, they have had in their mind. But this is not strange, and I am the last person to abuse the poets, since, apart from nature, they provide me with the chief pleasure I have in life.

It is a common experience of the artist with the brush to see effects in nature which he would never dream of attempting to transfer to canvas. They are beyond him—they are outside of the outermost limits of his art. So, too, there are things innumerable that mock the artist in words—even the inspired poet. Of all who have written, Keats has perhaps come nearest, on a few rare occasions, to an expression of the feeling which the visible world, in certain of its aspects and certain of its sights and sounds, inspires in us. That is the utmost—and how much is it? If any man can say that Keats has expressed all or as much as he has felt in nature or more than he has felt, I would say of such a man that he does not inhabit the same world with me, but lives in some other world.

CHAPTER IX

SUMMER HEAT

When the downs are most enjoyable—July in the wooded
lowland—The bliss of summer—Children's delight in heat—
Misery of cold—Piers Plowman—Langland's philosophy—
The happiest man in Sussex—A protection from the sun—
Heat not oppressive on the hills—Birds on Mount Harry—A
cup of cold water—Drawing water in a hat—Advantages of
a tweed hat—An unsympathetic woman—Beauty of
kindness.

The downs to my mind are most enjoyable during the eight or ten
hottest weeks of the year; not only because of the greater intensity of
life and colour at that season, but also because the heat of the sun,
always less oppressive than on the country below, and endurable
even at its greatest, as we had it in the exceptionally hot and dry
season of 1899, is at most times a positive pleasure. Midsummer
down on the level country makes us shade-lovers; here where the air
is more elastic we can rejoice to be in a shadeless land. And the
charm of the downs at this season, if by chance rain has fallen to
refresh and make them blossom, is never more appreciated than
when the visitor goes to them direct from the wooded district of the
weald. During the last half of July the woodland atmosphere weighs
somewhat heavily on the spirits. Month by month the colour has
deepened until it is almost sombre and resembles the everlasting
uniform green of a tropical forest. The tree-shaded bushes and briars,
the rank grasses, creepers, and weedy flowering plants, wear to our
anthropomorphic mind and vision something of a weary look; they
have felt the decay which is not yet apparent; the brightest blossoms
welcome us to their shady retreats with a somewhat pathetic smile.
Birds are more abundant than in spring, but they are mostly silent
and appear anxious to escape notice, slipping secretly away and
speaking to one another in low voices that have an unfamiliar sound.
It may even seem that there is something of mystery, or of
apprehension, in their infrequent subdued notes, which, they utter
involuntarily when disturbed; that they are prescient of coming
changes, and have even some dim knowledge of that long journey
from which so few will return to their places in spring; that they
have already begun to listen for the breath of autumn, rustling the
leaves with a sharper sibilant sound than that of summer. The

quietude reminds us of the sick-room; the hot, languid air is like a feverish breath that infects the blood. It is a joy to escape from such confinement, to go out into that lofty treeless world, into the glory of the sun that burns and does not hurt.

The power of the sun and its joy is not felt so early on the downs as on the lower country, and last season it was not until the middle of June that I experienced the blissful sensation and feeling in its fullness. Then a day came that was a revelation; I all at once had a deeper sense and more intimate knowledge of what summer really is to all the children of life; for it chanced that on that effulgent day even the human animal, usually regarded as outside of nature, was there to participate in the heavenly bounty. That I felt the happiness myself was not quite enough, unhuman, or uncivilised, as I generally am, and wish to be. High up the larks were raining down their brightest, finest music; not rising skyward nor falling earthward, but singing continuously far up in that airy blue space that was their home. The little birds that live in the furze, the titlarks, whitethroats, linnets, and stonechats, sprang upwards at frequent intervals and poured out their strains when on the wing. Each bird had its characteristic flight and gestures and musical notes, but all alike expressed the overflowing gladness that summer inspired, even as the flowers seemed to express it in their intense glowing colours; and as the butterflies expressed in their fluttering dances, and in the rapturous motions of their wings when at rest. There were many rabbits out, but they were not feeding, and when disturbed ran but fifteen or twenty yards away, then sat and looked at me with their big, round, prominent eyes, apparently too contented with life to suspect harm. But I saw no human creature in the course of a long ramble that morning until I was near the sea, when on approaching a coastguard station I all at once came upon some children lying on the grass on the slope of a down. There were five of them, scattered about, all lying on their backs, their arms stretched crossways, straight out, their hands open. It looked as if they had instinctively spread themselves out, just as a butterfly at rest opens wide its wings to catch the beams. The hot sun shone full on their fresh young faces; and though wide awake they lay perfectly still as I came up and walked slowly past them, looking from upturned face to face, each expressing perfect contentment; and as I successively caught their eyes they smiled, though still keeping motionless and silent as the bunnies that had regarded me a while before, albeit without smiling, Brer Rabbit being a serious little beast. Their quietude and composure in the presence of a stranger was unusual, and like the confidence of the wild rabbits on that day was caused by the delicious sensation of summer in the blood. We in our early years are little wild animals, and the wild animals are little children.

Cold, and the misery of cold have I known; cold of keen wind and bitter frost; cold of rain that rained every day where there was no fire to dry me, and no shelter; cold of long winter nights, spent shivering; and cold from hunger and thinness of blood. That was indeed what winter really meant to a majority of men, even in this long civilised land not so many centuries ago. These children reminded me of my own experiences in the past, and of the state of things in old times. For our little ones, even in this altered age in which we have made our own conditions, in their quick and keen response to nature's influences, perpetually recall our own past to us, and that of the race. The sight of their faces lit with the strong sunlight from above and the summer bliss from within, brought back the vision of old Piers Plowman, ill-fed and gaunt and ragged, following his plough on a winter's day—the picture which has often made me shiver with the sensation of remembered cold. Lines that had printed themselves indelibly on my memory, so keenly did I feel when I read them, now seemed all at once to have a new and deeper significance. "There the poor dare plead, " the old poet says; and by "there" he means after life and its miseries, at the Judgment-seat:

There the poor dare plead.
And prove by pure reson
To have allowance of his lord,
By the lawe he it claimeth:
Joye that never joye hadde
Of rightful jugge he asketh.
And seth, Lo, briddes and beasts.
That no blisse ne knoweth.
And wilde wormes in wodes,
Through winter thou them grievest
And maketh them well nigh meke
And mild for defaute;
And after thou sendeth them somer,
That is their sovereign joye
And blisse to all that ben
Both wilde and tame.

Note that this interpretation of Christ's teaching is not quite the same as ours, in these times of plenty. This old poet's philosophy is founded on the parable, literally taken, of Lazarus and Dives: you cannot have your sumptuous fare and purple and fine linen both here and hereafter. For all those whose portion in this life was perpetual toil and want and misery, and who bore it patiently (for patience was then the chief virtue), there was compensation after death. That was the law of the parable:

By the lawe he it claimeth.

It was only natural that the author of the Vision, living amid the conditions so hard for us to realise, which he describes, should have held such a belief, that it should seem "pure reson" to him. For He who rules over all is just even to the "briddes and beasts" and "wilde wormes in wodes. " With winter He grieves them and afterwards sends them summer; that is their bliss, the vital beams that gladden the stonechat and rabbit, and, piercing below the surface, unfreeze the torpid adder's blood. So, too, for poor humanity there is a glorious eternal summer after this life's bitter winter. This is the teaching of the Vision—poverty borne with patience is the best life, better and blesseder than riches:

For though it be sour to suffre
Thereafter cometh swete;
As on a walnut without
Is a bitter bark;
But after that bitter bark,
Be the shelle awaye.
Is a kernel of comfort
Kind to restore.

At the end of June, a fortnight after seeing the coastguard children, I was again vividly reminded of the bliss of summer "to all that ben" in an amusing way. It was an excessively hot morning, the hottest of the year so far, and I felt it all the more for being down in the valley of the Ouse, on a dusty flinty road, weary to walk in, between the little riverside villages of Southease and Rodmell. Here I spied a man coming towards me at a swinging pace; he was short and thick-set, aged about thirty, clad in old earth-coloured clothes, a small peakless cap thrust far back on his head, his broad face—the countenance of a genial ruffian—ashine with sweat and happiness. His swinging gait, jolly expression, and a bunch of freshly-pulled yellow flag lilies which he had stuck in the breast of his ragged old coat, plainly showed that he was no professional tramp. Yet he stopped me with a loud hearty greeting and the remark that it was splendid weather; then he added that he would be glad of a bit of bread and some beer at the next village, but was stony-broke. Now I had nothing but a florin in my pocket, and as my intention was to be out rambling all day I knew that I should badly want some money for refreshments before evening, and there was no place near to get change. I explained this to him, with apologies for not relieving his wants. "Oh, never mind, " he returned, "I'll manage to get to Newhaven. I've just come out, " he added. "I've been doing time over there"; here he jerked his thumb over his shoulder in the direction of Lewes. Then remarking again that it was a splendid day, and that he was very glad to be out once more, he bade me a hearty good-bye and went on his way to the coast. I looked after him, almost expecting to hear him burst out singing. He was probably the happiest man in Sussex on that hot morning. And no wonder, since coming out of gaol, whither he had perhaps been sent when the year was young, he had passed directly from the winter of his dim stone cell to summer in the fullness of its glory. He must indeed have been happy and seen all familiar things with a strange magical beauty in them, when he plucked those yellow flags to wear them as a big buttonhole! It was the only way in which he could express his overflowing joy, and love of life and liberty and of green mother earth; since he could not, like the resuscitated serpent, get himself a new shining garment for the occasion, nor like the wild bird sing a new wonderful song.

But the hottest season is after June—the season when, as I have said, the downs are to me most attractive. At this season my custom on going out on the hills is to carry a wetted pocket-handkerchief or piece of sponge in my hat: by renewing the moisture three or four times, or as often as water is found, I am able to keep my head perfectly cool during a ramble of ten or twelve hours on a cloudless day in July and August. Long ago, in South America, I discovered that the wet cloth was a great improvement on the cabbage-leaf, or thick fleshy leaf of some kind, which is universally used as a brain-protector. So long as the head is comfortable there is nothing to fear, the rest of the system being safeguarded by nature. Exercise keeps the body cool.

In the course of a hot summer day on these shadeless hills one may experience a variety of temperatures and a succession of contrasted sensations. Lying flat on the grass on a lower slope it is excessively hot; merely to sit or stand up is to enter into another and more temperate climate; in toiling up a steep slope the sensation is that of wading chin-deep in a hot bath with one's clothes on; higher up a breeze is often met which strikes one with a delicious chill. The sudden cold produced by rapid evaporation refreshes and exhilarates at the same time; it is like a draught of cider to the parched reaper. However motionless the air may be in the valleys, the deep clefts dividing the downs, there is always some wind on the summits.

There are of course some days in July and August when there is scarcely a breath of wind even on the highest crests; yet even so the heat is never so oppressive there. If at the height of 300 feet you feel that it would be a relief to creep into the shade of even a stunted blackthorn or furze-bush, at 800 feet you can still sit or even lie in the full blaze and enjoy it. Birds as well as men feel this; frequently on a hot windless day I have been surprised on getting to the highest point in any place at the number of birds collected on it; not to feed but merely to repose during the idle noonday hours. One August day, on coming to the summit of Mount Harry, west of Lewes, I found a company of rooks and daws not far short of a hundred, a large covey of red-legged partridges, many starlings, and about thirty missel-thrushes, all gathered at one spot on and near the big barrow on the hill top. I should have been glad to sit down quietly among them, but they would not have it so, birds having no power to distinguish those who wish for a "better friendship" with them; and so, some with a discontented caw or croak, others with whir of wings, and still others with harsh scolding notes, they all flew away in different directions, and left me with no companions except those wan people who are always with us and look less substantial than ever in the strong sunlight; and with nothing to think about but an old unhappy thing; how on "that dim day of light, " May 14, 1264, dead bodies covered the ground, and gasping and groaning was heard on every side; and either was desirous of bringing the other out of life, and the father spared not the sonne, nor the sonne the father, and Christian blood was shed without pitie on all that green solitary hill.

The shepherd of the downs, out for the day in summer, has a provision against thirst in his can of water or cold tea, which is usually kept concealed in a furze-bush. To carry water is a precaution which I never take, because, for one reason, I love not to be encumbered with anything except my clothes. Even my glasses, which cannot be dispensed with, are a felt burden. Then, too, I always expect to find a cottage or farm somewhere; and the water when obtained is all the more refreshing when really wanted; and finally the people I meet are interesting, and but for thirst I should never know them.

That ancient notion of the value of a cup of cold water, and the merit there is in giving it, is not nearly dead yet in spite of civilisation. Water is the one thing it is still more blessed to give than to receive; and if you approach any person wearing on your face the look of one about to ask for some benefit, and your request is for a drink of water, you are sure to make him happy. This is not said cynically: if by chance one of our millionaire dukes has ever in his life given a drink of water to some poor, very thirsty man, he will secretly know that this action on his part gave him more happiness than it did to build a cathedral, or give a park to the public, or to win the blue ribbon of the turf, or even to be Prime Minister.

On one excessively sultry breathless morning, when I had foolishly gone out for a long ramble without my usual protection for the head, I all at once began about noon to suffer intolerably from both heat and thirst. I was probably below par on that day, for I had never felt more parched, even when travelling for twelve hours in the sun without a drink of water; and as to the heat, I experienced that most miserable sensation of a boiling brain—a feeling which associates itself in the mind with the image of a pot boiling on the fire, bubbling and puffing out jets of steam. The nearest inhabited place in sight was a small farmhouse on the crest of a hill about two and a half miles away, with deep hollows and hills to descend and ascend between. But down below me, at the bottom of the valley, not much more than half a mile from where I stood, there was a small, half-ruined, barn-like building, and not far from the building a shepherd was standing watching his flock. To him I went and asked if any water was to be had at that place. He shook his head. "No well there? " I said, indicating the old stone building. "Oh, yes, there's an old well there; you can drag the stone off, but you can't get any water without a bottle and string. " The fellow's indifference irritated me, and turning my back on him I went and hunted for the well, and succeeded in dragging aside the heavy stone that covered it, to find that the water was not more than about seven feet below the surface. Twisting the band of my tweed hat in the crook of my stick handle, then lying so as to hang well over the edge, I managed to fish up a hatful of water, and drank the whole of it, much to the shepherd's amusement, who had followed me to watch operations.

The water was delightfully cold and refreshing, and the well-soaked hat, when I put it on, kept my head cool for the rest of the day.

My hat of an unsuitable material had proved directly useful in that case. The straw hat is of course lighter and cooler than any other; but no person with any consideration for the feelings of a bird in the matter would think of wearing it, any more than he would think of sporting white or light-coloured flannels. White and black are equally bad for those who go a-birding. There is nothing like tweeds of a greyish-brown indeterminate colour, with a tweed hat to match.

A second amusing adventure, which I had at a farm in a deep hollow in the midmost part of the South Down range, where it is broadest, remains to be told. The small grey old house, shaded by old trees, so far removed from the noise of the world in that deep valley among the great hills, had enchanted me when I first beheld it, and hearing later that the people of the house sometimes took lodgers in summer, I went to inquire. I left the village north of the downs where I was staying a little after seven o'clock in the morning, and after being out on the hills for over six hours in a great heat, visiting many furzy places in my ramble, I went down to that shady peaceful spot where I hoped to find a home. Some old trees grew on the lawn, and on a chair in the shade sat a grey-haired man in broadcloth clothes, his feet in red carpet-slippers, looking very pale and ill. He was, I supposed, a visitor or guest, and a town man; probably a prosperous tradesman out of health, too old to make any change in the solemn black respectable dress he had always worn on Sundays and holidays. Going on to the open front door I knocked, and after a time my summons was answered by the landlady, a person of a type to be met with occasionally not in Sussex only but all over the country, the very sight of which causes the heart to sink; a large, heavy-bodied, slow-minded, and slow-moving middle-aged woman, without a gleam of intelligence or sympathy in her big expressionless face; a sort of rough-hewn pre-adamite lump of humanity, or gigantic land-tortoise in petticoats. When questioned, she said No, she could not take me in. Yes, she took lodgers and had a party now; they were going, but then another party had engaged to come. She never took but one party at a time—that was her way. Cross-questioned, she said that it didn't matter whether it was a single man who was out every day and all day long or a family of a dozen, so long as it was one party. She laid herself out to do for one party at a time, and had never taken more and couldn't think of taking two—it upset her.

Very well, that point was decided against me; it was now time to say that I had been out walking in the sun for over six hours and was hungry and thirsty and tired—could she give me something to eat while I rested? No, she could not; it was hard to get anything in such an out-of-the-way place, and the provisions in the house were no more than were needed. Oh, never mind, I returned, some bread and cheese will do very well—I'm very hungry. But there was no bread and cheese to spare, she said. Then, I said, I must make a drink of milk do. There was no milk, said she, or so little that if she gave me any they would be short. Then, I said, getting cross, perhaps you will be so good as to give me a drink of water. She revolved this last request in her dull brain for a minute or so, then saying that she could do that, slowly went away to the kitchen to get the water.

During our colloquy another person, a well-dressed elderly woman, the wife of the man in broadcloth and slippers, had come into the hall and listened. She now dived into her rooms, and in a very few moments returned with as much bread and cheese as a hungry man could eat on a plate; then taking the glass of water from the landlady's hand, she insisted on carrying the plate and the glass out to the lawn, where I could rest in the shade while eating. The other woman had meanwhile stared in an uncomprehending way, the dull surprise in her look gradually changing to something resembling admiration. What a strange thing it was that her lady lodger had popped into the hall, listened like a robin to half a dozen words, and understood the whole matter in a flash; and that though it was no concern of hers, and she had been asked for nothing, and had her own anxieties and her ailing husband to attend to, she had in an instant supplied my wants. And not only that, she had added pleasant words, spoken quite naturally in a nice voice, just as if I had been someone belonging to her instead of a rough-looking stranger. Now she, ponderous earthy soul that she was, could not have spoken in that tone if she had practised the trick for fifty years. Truly her lodger was a wonderful woman!

While eating my lunch I got into conversation with the man in broadcloth and slippers, his wife meanwhile coming and going, now with a cushion for his head or something else for his comfort, or only to flit round us in a bird-like way and see how we were getting on. But when I had finished the water and went back for more, she met me in the hall with a bottle of ginger-beer. Now that is a drink which I care not for on account of its mawkishness, but on this occasion the taste was delicious; and even its whitish colour, which had always been unpleasant to my sight, now looked beautiful, and was caused by a mixture of that precious fluid which is more refreshing and gladdening to the heart than purple wine or any other drink.

CHAPTER X

SWALLOWS AND CHURCHES

Abundance of swallows in downland villages—The swallow's batlike faculty—Old house at Ditchling—Church owls and Ditchling Church—Shingled spires—Pleasure of finding churches open—A strange memorial in a downland church—A nap in West Firle churchyard—Slow-worms in churchyards—Increase of swallows at Ditchling—House-martins on telegraph wires—The telegraph a benefit to birds—Telegraph poles in the landscape—Sound of telegraph wires—A cockney's bird-lore—A Sussex man on swifts—Swifts rising from a flat surface—The swift mystery—Swifts at Seaford—A Somerset bird-boy's strange story.

The down country appears to have a great attraction for the swallow, house-martin, and swift. One must group these three together. The last is swallow-like in his appearance and aerial habits, and to the popular mind is, and always will be, a swallow. It may be that the causes which have resulted in a decrease in the number of these birds in many other parts of the country are local, and have not affected this district. At all events, during the last few years these species, although declining elsewhere, have been exceedingly abundant in the villages and hamlets among and at the foot of the downs. At some spots where they most abounded, looking down on the village from a high window or other elevation, the effect was produced of a multitude of bees or other insects, flying about over a hive or some such centre of attraction, so numerous were the birds. Among the villages, Alfriston and Ditchling appeared to be the most favoured by swallows and martins. At the former I counted thirteen martins' mud nests stuck to the wall of a small cottage opposite to the house I was staying at. These nests and some hundreds more were occupied, and mostly had young birds in them; yet more nests were being made, and if a woman came out of her front door and emptied a bucket of dirty water in the road, half a dozen martins would quickly drop down on the wet place to get a little mortar for the nests they were building. The ancient chimneys and picturesque red-tiled roofs of the houses were as attractive to the swallows as the walls under the eaves to the martins. The birds were in hundreds. Sitting at a front window, while waiting for my breakfast, the air seemed full of swallows whirling about like house-flies in a room, and of the sound of their voices. Presently another sound was heard, something between a rumbling and a fluttering, and down the chimney into the room flew or tumbled a swallow. I closed the window and tried to catch it to put it out, but the poor bird flew wildly about the room and I could not get near it. Now I noticed that although the two well-cleaned windows at the front were in appearance two patches of shining light and open ways to liberty, the bird in all his wild flights about the large dim room never touched them. Almost any other bird would have instantly dashed himself against the glass. Tired of the vain chase, I finally put up one sash of a window and sat down: at once the captive, doubtless feeling a way of escape in the more elastic air coming to it from that direction, flew straight from the other side of the room and passed out. Its action appeared to show that the swallow, in spite of its feathery covering, has an almost bat-like sensitiveness to enable it in unusual circumstances to avoid striking against any object in its flight. It has been observed that bats flying round in a dimly-lighted room were not deceived by the light coming through a pane of glass; but, on the other hand, they would flutter before a keyhole or any other small aperture through which a current of out-door air could come. This exquisite sensitiveness of the bat's wing, which is nerve as well as organ of flight, is a corrective of vision, which is liable in all creatures to deception. That the swallow, too, should be found possessed of this additional sense, came to me as a surprise.

At Ditchling the extraordinary abundance of swallow and swift life interested me more than the ancient traditional yarns about Alfred the Great's connection with the village; and, a long time after, that of Anne of Cleves (poor thing!) who, as a divorced lady, appears to have inhabited a good many houses in these parts. The church of this same village is greatly admired by artists as well as by antiquarians; it also possessed that which to my mind made it the most perfect sacred edifice in all the downs district—namely, a family of white owls, strictly protected by the parson, tamer than most birds of their kind.

The nest, or breeding-hole, was under the eaves, and after the young were hatched, every evening just when the sun went down behind the great round hills, strange noises would begin to issue from the hole; —sounds as of a sleeper with a bad cold in his head, uncomfortably breathing through his nose, prolonged, sibilant, and tremulous, and occasionally deeper as if in imitation of the death-rattle in a human throat. These noises were uttered by the young birds, crying for their tea, or breakfast, or whatever we like to call their first meal. And presently the old owls would shuffle out to fly about the village in their usual flopping, unballasted, aimless manner, this way and that, seemingly at random as if they had lost their steering intelligence. But in twenty minutes to half an hour one would be back from the neighbouring rickyard with a mouse in his claws.

Seated on one of the lichen-stained tombstones, or in a chair on a small lawn abutting on the churchyard, each evening while waiting for the owls to come out, I found my sight resting with a rare and untiring pleasure on the church before me; so perfect a building it was of its kind, so well placed on its mound with the old red-tiled houses harmoniously grouped about it, and so noble a background had the picture in the great round darkening hills and the luminous evening sky.

There is a strong family resemblance in the churches of this district: they are small in small villages, built of stone or flint, with low square towers surmounted by small shingled spires. Wood and stone have the same grey colour of age and weather, and the exposed wood has the appearance of being perdurable as the stone. It is indeed long-lasting, the shingles being made of hard butt oak and pinned with oak wood, or fastened with copper nails. In long, excessively dry summers, like that of 1899, the shingles shrink and grow loose, and rattle in the hot violent winds so loudly that a person up in the belfry might imagine that their time had nearly come, that a mightier blast will by-and-by tear them off, to whirl them away like thistle-down and scatter them wide over the country. Such a fear would be idle; they rattle but keep their hold until the rain comes to soak and tighten them in their places; and they will still be there in all weathers when we that see them and think about their mutations shall no longer be sensible to summer's heat and winter's wet and cold.

I forget who it was who said of some peaceful village churchyard that it made one in love with death to be in such a place. That is a feeling which may be experienced in some of the villages here—Wilmington, Berwick, and West Firle, for instance. Ditchling churchyard is too high above the surrounding level, and unshaded with trees, to allow of such a fancy. Often during a long walk over the downs in hot weather I have thought of the church and churchyard before me as of a shaded fountain in a parched desert. Arrived at the place I have gone straight to the church, and am happy to say that in many instances I have found it open "for private meditation and prayer. " When on such occasions I find the door locked against me, then the building is no longer what it was originally intended for, and sacred, but is that inhospitable place where a cup of cold water was refused me when I was athirst, and my only wish is for a piece of red chalk to set a mark upon it.

Coming from the burning heat and glare of noon, how grateful the coolness and how beautiful the rich everlasting twilight of the interior seem! It is in the ancient peaceful village church, of all houses made with hands, that one can know that perfect rest and contentment, the peace which passeth understanding, experienced in our communings with nature, where nature has not been marred by man.

Only on one occasion did I experience feelings very different from those I have described, in a downland church, which I found open one day at noon, my favourite hour. On taking a seat about the middle of the church, I noticed that there was but one memorial in it—a mural tablet of enormous size—on the wall at my right, lettered from top to bottom; but for some time I paid no attention to it. By-and-by, turning my sight that way, the huge solitary marble with the big inscription arrested my attention and I began to read, first with but slight curiosity, almost mechanically, then with surprise and amusement, and when I got to the end, for the first time in my life I burst out laughing in a church. This is what I read:

NEAR THIS PLACE LIES INTERRED
THOMAS JOHNSON
WHO DEPARTED THIS LIFE AT CHARLTON
DECEMBER 2OTH, 1744.
FROM HIS EARLY INCLINATION TO FOXHOUNDS
HE SOON BECAME AN EXPERIENCED HUNTSMAN.
HIS KNOWLEDGE IN THE PROFESSION, WHEREIN HE
HAD NO SUPERIOR, AND HARDLY AN EQUAL,
JOINED TO HIS HONESTY IN EVERY OTHER PARTICULAR,
RECOMMENDED HIM TO THE SERVICE, AND GAIN'D
HIM THE APPROBATION OF SEVERAL OF THE NOBILITY
AND GENTRY. AMONG THESE WERE THE LORD CONWAY,
EARL OF CARDIGAN, THE LORD GOWER, THE DUKE
OF MARLBOROUGH, AND THE HONOURABLE M. SPENCER.

THE LAST MASTER WHOM HE SERVED, AND IN WHOSE SERVICE
HE DIED, WAS CHARLES DUKE OF RICHMOND
LENNOX AND AUBIGNY, WHO ERECTED THIS MONUMENT
TO THE MEMORY OF A GOOD AND FAITHFUL SERVANT
AS A REWARD TO THE DECEASED
AND AN INCITEMENT TO THE LIVING.
Go thou and do likewise.—St. Luke, chap. X. ver. xxxvii.
Here Johnson lies. What Hunter can deny
Old honest TOM *the tribute of a sigh?*
Deaf is the Ear, which caught the opening sound,
Dumb is that Tongue, which cheered the Hills around.
Unpleasing Truth, Death hunts us from our Birth,
In view, and Men, like Foxes, take to Earth.

Even now, when I think of that village in the West Sussex Downs, and remember the effect the inscription in its church produced on me when I first saw it, I am teased with a sudden impulse to explode. But though I laughed I was not pleased, and to amusement succeeded disgust; for even those who are without reverence, and are mockers at religion, do because of their humanity yet reverence one saying and one parable of Christ, and think with unconscious worship that those were beautiful and sacred words used by Him on that occasion, which are here put to so degraded a use. The church, even before I left it, had ceased to be a sacred building. There might be something there to interest the archaeologist; to me it was only old Tom Johnson's house, and was no better than the village ale-house to sit and rest in.

No such feeling have I experienced in any other downland church; and into how many of them, all along the range, from Pevensey to the Hampshire border, have I entered to find rest and refreshment in burning summer weather!

Cooled in blood and brain, I pass out from the dim church to the churchyard; and however deeply shaded by old trees it may be, the moving air and green tempered sunlight strike me with a new, keen, instant pleasure, as if I had just escaped from confinement in an underground cell or vault. On such occasions I am less in love with death than with sleep.

I remember that in the cool shady churchyard at Firle, lying under a tree on a thick brown and green turf, soothed by the musical sounds of blackbird and blackcap, I fell into a very pleasant doze, and that when my eyes began gradually to open they rested on a silvery-grey sinuous streak on the grass, close to my face. First I took it for a ribbon, then a cord, and at last it dawned on me that it was a poor little sham serpent, with the adder's black mark on its belly, on which, adder-like, it is compelled to go; but its back silvery grey, to symbolise its dove-like innocence. So motionless was it that I thought it dead, or else that the drowsy peaceful spirit of the place had breathed upon us both. But when I picked it up it woke too, quickly enough, and was glad, when I grew tired of playing with it, to be released.

It struck me at the time as a curious coincidence that my last meeting with a slow-worm before this one at Firle was also in a churchyard. This occurred two months earlier in the season, at Boldre, in the New Forest. Coming out of church after Sunday morning service, I went with a party of young girls to look at Gilpin's tomb in the churchyard. Pushing some ivy growing against the stone aside we disturbed the little silvery snake, who appeared to have made a home of the grand old Forest parson's last resting-place.

From churches, owls, and snakes (or lizards) let us return to the subject of swallows. At Ditchling I believe the house-martins were rather more than twice as numerous as the chimney-swallows. In August some idea of the rapid increase that was going on in the former species could be had, owing to the habit of the young birds of congregating on the telegraph wires in the village. There were four wires, and at one spot in the middle of the village one lot of the young birds would crowd the wires for a length of forty or fifty yards. This crowd numbered about 300; I counted them, and they always, when they settled on the wires, occupied the same spot, and in about the same numbers. A short distance away, at the end of the village street, a second lot, numbering about 150, would congregate. There were no chimney-swallows in these two crowds: it was rare even to see more than two or three adult martins among the young birds. The two gatherings were composed of martins bred in the village, and now able to take care of themselves: the parent birds were all occupied in hatching more eggs and feeding more young— second and third broods. Here, then, were 450 house-martins reared in the village by the middle of August; and as breeding would go on for five or six weeks longer, at least 150 more birds would be reared, making an increase of 600 in this species for the season. The chimney-swallows would rear altogether not less than 200 young, so that the total swallow increase would be at least 800.

The young martins were very tame, and were a pretty and interesting ornament of the village, attracting a good deal of attention even from the most stolid of the natives, as they sat preening their feathers and dozing in the hot sun, rows on rows of birds above the noisy little street, seen sharply against that ever cloudless bright blue summer sky.

Lying in bed at five o'clock in the morning I could see and admire them, as they were directly before and on a level with my open bedroom window. Very early one morning a half-dressed, dirty-looking little boy rushed out of the cottage opposite, and seizing hold of a passing dog began to tease and drag it about; the dog after a few minutes escaped out of his hands and ran away. Then the naughty boy, looking round for something else to exercise his energies on, caught sight of the crowd of martins high above him, and began to shout at them to make them fly. Then he tried to climb up by one of the posts, but always after getting up a few feet slipped down. His next move was to get a stick and beat loudly on the telegraph pole, and when all these efforts had failed he fell to shouting again, and shouted and yelled so loudly and persistently that his mother, crazed by the noise, at length rushed forth and hunted him in. The martins had quietly sat out the whole performance.

It is curious to see in rural districts how the telegraph line from being, like the lighthouse, a danger to birds, killing and maiming considerable numbers, has in time grown to be an advantage to them, affording a convenient perch and lofty look-out which many species habitually prefer to trees and bushes. It has become *natural* to them, as if we had supplied a real want in their lives, an omission of nature. So, too, it is curious to note that the long line of tall straight poles and suspended wires, which one would imagine to be nothing but a disfigurement to the landscape, fit into it at many points so admirably as to be an improvement, a positive beauty in the scene, reminding one of those tall guide-posts with a crosspiece near the top to be found on some of the extensive tidal flats on our sea coast. The upright pole and the flagstaff, and even the lower finger-posts and the slender stone cross in many villages, produce an effect like that of the slim Lombardy poplar in the landscape and please the eye. The gibbet, too, in vanished days doubtless had a similar aesthetic value.

Breath of Christian charity.
Blow, and sweep it from the earth!

shouted the poet; but who in these days, in spite of charity, would not welcome back this ancient ornament to the landscape, if it could but be used to suspend our universally abhorred scorchers by the neck until they were dead, dead, dead, and food for crows and pies?

In its sound, too, the rural telegraph line appeals to the aesthetic sense; it is a harp and mysterious voice in the desert and in all solitary silent places. I remember, years ago, in South America, seeing a group of natives standing and listening to the tremulous musical hum that rose and fell with the wind, and hearing them gravely say that they could hear the voices of men sending messages and talking to each other over long distances, but could not make out what they were saying. Even for us there is a slight something of mystery in the swelling and dying tones, and the sound is in itself beautiful and very natural. It closely resembles that most musical and human-like sound of insect life, which may be heard in many spots on the high downs in July and August; a sound of innumerable bees and honey-eating flies in the flowering heather, their individual small voices blended into one loud continuous hum that rises, too, and falls with the wind. A man led blindfolded over the downs to one of these flowery places, and standing there in the hot breeze, would probably think that he was listening to the harp of the tall wooden pole and suspended wires.

I noticed that in some of the villages in the downs there were no swifts; in other villages and in the coast towns they were abundant. It was not uncommon to see as many as thirty or forty swifts rushing about in the air together, and the downs district generally appeared to be as favourable to these birds as to the swallows. At one village, one morning, I was standing in a garden watching the numbers of swifts, swallows, and martins peopling the air overhead. When my host came out to me I called his attention to the birds. "I call them all swallows, " he said, and in spite of all I could say on the subject he assured me that he could see no difference between swift, chimney-swallow, and house-martin. "Are you a native of this place? " I asked. "Oh no, I was born within sound of Bow Bells, " he returned with pride. That explained his invincible ignorance. But the

Sussexian, though he knows a great deal more than a cockney, also makes some funny mistakes. One day at Lewes I noticed a lot of swifts, about twenty-four birds, rushing round and round in their usual mad way, and at each turn coming down and passing so close to the gable of a stone house, a public school near the station, as to touch the stone wall a yard or two below the roof with their wings. At intervals after five or six rushes they would scatter all about the sky, then in a minute or two gather and resume their mad flight over the same aerial racecourse, touching the wall again each time as they swept by. I presently noticed that half a dozen workmen, standing close by in a group, were also observing the birds and talking about them. "I wonder what these mad birds are after? " I said, going up to the men. One of them undertook to enlighten me. "They are swifts, " he said, "but here we call them Black Jacks. They are after insects—that's what they feed on. I mean flies, " he kindly explained. He then went on to say that when swifts are seen rushing round in a bunch at one spot it is because flies are most abundant there, and that the birds catch many more flies than they can eat. He once saw a swift fluttering on the ground, unable to rise, and picking it up he found that flies were swarming all over it. So many flies had this swift caught and put there in its feathers that the weight of them had borne it down to the ground. I ventured to tell him that he was wrong, that the flies he had seen swarming in the plumage of a fallen swift were parasitical on the bird, and that the swift was probably in poor condition and so much infested and tormented by the insects as to be unable any longer to fly. My man looked gravely at me but said nothing, and I took his silence to mean that he did not believe the parasite story, or was not pleased at being put right about his familiar Black Jacks in the presence of his comrades, who were not ornithologists.

The old belief that the swift, when by chance he comes down, is unable to rise from a flat surface owing to the length of his wings, is, I think, well-nigh obsolete, although one does occasionally hear it. Swifts get many a fall in spring, and are often to be seen getting up again from the ground. During the last ten or fifteen years starlings have increased enormously all over the country. They are liked better than formerly, and are not shot so much nor driven away from their roosting-places in winter, nor are they used much now for trap-shooting—a form of sport which has been long declining. One result of this increase of starlings is that the bird is becoming especially numerous in the towns and villages, and that in April he takes possession of the swift's breeding-holes under the eaves of cottages, and similar situations. The swifts, on their arrival in May, find themselves dispossessed of their holes, and fight to recover them. Then in the early mornings you may see swifts and starlings falling from the eaves clenched together, and, when on the ground, separating and rising up to renew the combat at the entrance to the hole.

The swift question, which interests naturalists at the present time, is the habit of the bird, or of the males when breeding is in progress, of rising up higher and higher in the air at a late hour in the evening until they disappear from sight, and finally cease to be heard. It is supposed that these mounting birds, who are not seen to return, although it is possible that they do return after dark, spend the night at a vast height rushing or sailing about in the air, and that with morning they return.

In the evening, when there are eggs or young in the nest, it may be observed that the females are out feeding and rushing about with their mates, and that the males drive them back to the nests before going off themselves for their supposed night out. For some evenings in June, at Seaford, where the swifts were very numerous, I watched this interesting performance, and it was curious and amusing to see a pair in some cases, the hen-bird wildly rushing away, the mate in mad pursuit, and then when with infinite pains she had been driven home suddenly dashing off again, and the wild chase about the sky beginning afresh. Once I saw the hen-bird break away four times after being brought to the breeding-hole; but after the fourth time she remained in the nest, and the good zealous husband went away to enjoy himself. A swift chasing his wife home in the evening can easily be distinguished from one swift chasing another swift for fun, or whatever the motive is that keeps them in a perpetual hunt after one another. He follows her closely in all her mad flights and sudden doublings until he has got her face towards home, and then keeping close to her agitates his wings in a peculiar manner, at intervals gliding smoothly, uttering all the time a measured sharp clicking chirp—a sound as of repeated strokes on a piece of metal.

In Somerset I heard a curious little story which may prove of interest to those who are accustomed to watch the flight of the swifts on summer evenings with the object of finding out their secret.

One April evening, near Wells, I was sauntering along a road separated from a copse by an old moss-grown stone wall, when I noticed a boy moving cautiously about in the deep shadows of the trees, and watching me suspiciously.

"Found any nests? " I called out suddenly to him. He very quickly replied that he was not looking for nests, and had seen none; then he added that he was looking for primroses. Now he had no primroses in his hands, and as a matter of fact none grew in that particular copse; but I did not point this out to him, being desirous of engaging him in conversation. He was a singular-looking boy, about fourteen to fifteen years old; very thin, with long legs, small head, and sharp round face, and was dressed in earth-coloured, threadbare clothes much too small for him. With that small sharp face and those shifty eyes under his little grey cap, he looked curiously like some furred creature—rat or vole, with perhaps a dash of stoat in his composition, and if his nose had been longer I might have added that there was even a touch of the shrew-mouse in his appearance.

After I had been standing there speaking to him for a little while he got over his distrust, and coming out of the shadow of the trees climbed upon the wall, and sitting there became quite talkative, and told me all about his life and the wild creatures he had observed. He was a farm labourer's son, and his birthplace and home was high up on the Mendips, in the ancient desolate village of Priddy, a few miles from Wells. Since he was big enough to run about he had been employed as a bird-scarer on the farm where his father worked, and he appeared to have been an extremely observant boy. Talking of swifts he said, "They screechers be curious birds: did you ever hear, zur, that they be up flying about all night and come back in the marning? "

I asked him if someone had told him that, and he said No, he had found it out himself. Morning after morning he had noticed, just after sunrise, that a number of swifts suddenly made their appearance at the same spot, not far from a field that he had to watch. The birds would appear first at a great height, and rush straight down as if falling from the sky, until within a few yards of the earth, when they would dash off in various directions or begin flying about the village. It came into his head to play them a trick, and one morning he took the loaded gun, used for scaring the rooks, and stationed himself a little before sunrise at the spot where the swifts invariably made their descent. Shortly after sunrise they appeared, first as small specks in the sky, coming down with tremendous speed; and waiting until they were within thirty yards of his head he fired his gun into the middle of the bunch. Instantly the birds scattered, but after a few moments came together again and began to mount higher and higher until they disappeared from sight in the sky, and he saw no more of them until a later hour in the day.

It struck me as extremely improbable that this most circumstantial story was invented by the boy; in any case, perhaps it would be as well if those who are accustomed to watch the swifts rising on a summer evening until they disappear from sight, and to listen to their shrill triumphant screams growing fainter and fainter until they cease to be audible, would also watch for their return at sunrise in the morning.

CHAPTER XI

AUTUMN

Suddenness of the change from summer to autumn on the downs—Birds in autumn—Meadow-pipits—Shore birds on the hills—September flowers—Remnant of insect-life—Effect of rough weather—Effect on the mind of the cessation of life—Man's long life—An immortal surveying the insect tribes of human kind—The prospect from the hills—Pleasure of walking.

On the South Downs the change from summer to autumn is almost startling in its suddenness. The rough September days of wind and driving rain, and of nights when the temperature drops almost to freezing point, make little difference in the lower sheltered country; flowers fade and life lessens gradually there, and from August onwards the change is scarcely perceptible until in October the autumnal colours begin to appear in the trees. On the treeless hills the effect of a spell of rough weather with a touch of winter in it is infinitely greater: you are astonished at the almost total absence of life and colour, the naked cheerless aspect of things: September is then like December.

Succeeding warm days bring back a little of the lost bloom, and birds increase again; —rooks, starlings, missel-thrushes, and some others that were driven away by the bad weather now return to their old feeding-grounds. Migrants and wanderers, too, appear in limited numbers; small parties of wheatears, stonechats, and pied wagtails. The most numerous of these travellers that camp on the downs are the meadow-pipits. Everywhere on the sheep-walks you come upon their scattered flocks, looking like a lot of mice creeping about on the turf. They have a thin little chirping note as they fly from you—a slight sorrowful sound, yet distinctly reminiscent of their tinkling fairy-like summer song.

Another melancholy but wilder and more musical bird-sound to be heard on the high downs is the cry of migrating shore birds, dotterels and sandpipers as a rule. They are seen in flocks of two or three dozen to a hundred or more, sometimes associating with starlings and feeding among the scattered sheep. It is a beautiful cry which they utter as they rise to wheel about in a small cloud over the green down, changing from grey to white, and white to grey. That wild, clear, inflected note has the sound and smell and freshness of ocean in it.

In warm weather you may look again for flowers: yellow patches of dwarf whin, and here and there among the browns and dull greens a glowing bunch of the small-leafed heath or the paler purple ling. Most summer flowers in fact linger on into or bloom again in September. On a mullein stalk covered with dry seed-vessels you will find a solitary blossom; the honeysuckle has a few blooms, pale and scentless: and here and there all over the downs you will find, "blooming alone, " the dwarf thistle, hawkweed, rockrose, bedstraw, milfoil, viper's bugloss, harebell, thyme, sweet woodruff, and many more. The scabious, both blue and mauve, is perhaps the commonest flower at this season; and the minute delightful eyebright, the most abundant in certain spots where the soil is thinnest and the turf scarcely covers the underlying chalk. But night by night the year is busy with her cold fingers picking these last gems out of her mantle—the ornaments that accord not with her faded cheeks and sorrowful eyes.

Greatest of all seems the change with regard to insect life: but a few days ago you moved in a world teeming with millions of brilliant active beings, so numerous and small and swift in their motions as to be "seen rather than distinguished. " And now? —Well, if the wind is still and the sun shines and you miss and look for them, you will find a few left: a bumble-bee mechanically going about on his rounds with a listless flight and the merest ghost of his old hum; a songless grasshopper; a solitary fly trying to appear cheerful. You look in vair. for the merry little blue butterflies and the grey heaths, so numerous a little while ago. It is a surprise to see so splendid a creature as the red admiral: he is one of a second brood, and has come too late into his inheritance and will not keep it long. For the rest you will see an occasional common white, or a small heath; or your sight may be attracted by a spot of glowing colour on the sunny side of a gorse bush—a small copper with open wings basking and bathing in the vital heat and light, perhaps for the last time, before day comes to a chilly end.

Even these few survivors may not remain long; the September sunshine is very sweet and pleasant to behold, and may last many days; but it is never confidently looked for, and would not seem half so sweet if it could be expected to last. After golden days the grey come again, and the wind blows everlastingly; the high hill-tops are once more barren and bleak, and you are glad to come into rough brambly places, where all wild winged life that has not been blown away has hidden itself from the blast. But how little it is! Perhaps you will see a yellowhammer rush out of its hiding-place and perch on a bush-top near to see what creature has disturbed it. There for a few moments it will sit, swayed about, its feathers roughed, its long tail blown over its back or to the side at right angles with its body—a picture of discomfort. You may think that on such a day more may be seen by sitting still in the shelter of a bush than by roaming; you may sit for an hour, or for hours, and see nothing, and hear nothing—not an echo of any summer note. Nothing but the wind sweeping through the yellow bents with a long scythe-like sound, rising in gusty moments to a loud sharp hiss.

On such a day of silence and desolation a remembrance of the late summer has come back suddenly like a lightning-flash to my mind, with such startling vividness as to affect me powerfully. A vision of the vanished insect life that a little while ago covered these green flowering hills. I moved and had my being amid that life as in a golden mist spread over the earth; my ears were full of the noise of innumerable fine small voices blending into one voice; wheresoever I looked their minute swift-moving bodies appeared as thin dark lines on the air and over the green surface. Forms so infinitely varied, yet so wonderfully fashioned, each aglow with its complete separate life, and all in harmony with all life and all nature, responsive in a million secret springs to each and every external influence; so well balanced in their numerous parts and perfect in their equipment, so intense in their lives as to seem fitted to endure for ever. And now in so short a time, in a single day and night as it seems, it is all over, the feast and fairy-dance of life; the myriads of shining gem-like bodies turned to dead dust, the countless multitude of brilliant little individual souls dissipated into thin air and blown whithersoever the wind blows!

The first and inevitable effect of such a thought, when the tremendous tragedy of the passing year is brought unexpectedly and vividly before the mind, compressed into a moment of time, is a profound melancholy, as of a black shadow of apprehension coming over the soul. But it is like a shadow on the earth on a day of flying cloud and broken sunshine that is quickly gone. That teeming life of yesterday has indeed vanished from our sight for ever; it is nothing now, and its place will know it no more; but extinction came not on it before the seeds of the life that is to be were sown—small and abundant as the rust-coloured seed of the mullein, that looked like inorganic dust, and was shaken out of its dead cups by the blast and scattered upon the ground. Or smaller still, like the infinitesimal particles enclosed within the round case of the dead fungus of the downs—the devil's snuff-box of the peasant—which, when trodden upon, or broken by a blow of a stick, sends out a dense purple or deep yellow vapour, which floats away in the wind and vanishes. The still earth is full of it. Out of the matted roots of the turf and from the grey soil beneath, innumerable forms of life resembling those that have vanished will spring to light—creatures of a thousand beautiful shapes, lit with brilliant colour, intense in their little lives, for ever moving in a passionate, swift, fantastic dance.

And we shall see it all again, and in seeing renew the old familiar pleasure. For these innumerable little lives quickly pass while ours endure. Furthermore, the brief life which they have is but one, and though their senses be brilliant they see not beyond their small horizons. To us the Past and the Future are open, like measureless countries of diversified aspect, lying beyond our horizon; yet we may see them and are free to range over them at will. It may even happen that the autumnal spectacle of the cessation of life on the earth, nature's yearly tragedy, brought thus suddenly and sharply before the mind's eye, may cause us to realise for the first time what this freedom of the mind really means. It multiplies our years and makes them so many that it is a practical immortality. A vivid consciousness of it, coming thus suddenly, puts the soul in a proud temper, and we all at once begin to abhor the sickly teachings of those who see in nature's mutations, in cloud and wind and rain and the fall of the leaf, and the going out of ephemeral life, nothing but mournful messages, dreary symbols, reminders of our mortality. It is a false, debilitating doctrine which they preach and sing; an ancient fable, a tale of a bogie invented a thousand years ago to frighten unruly children and make them good. We are rather of the Psalmist's virile mind, when he said that those who had compassed him round, and had come to him like bees, were extinct as the fire under the thorns; and then triumphantly cried, "*I* shall not die, but live! "

Let us imagine a god, or immortal being of some kind, in a reverie, seated on some great hill—Caburn, or Firle, or Cissbury—seeing as in a vision the "insect tribes of human kind" that have dwelt upon these green downs since the coming of man—Saxon, and Dane, and Roman, and Briton, and the earlier races that were slain by the Celt, and the earlier still, and others and still others further back in time. All the events of long thousands of years, all the thousands of "generations of deciduous men, " called back and seen passing in procession before that clear cold immortal mind. Dark and pale races, speaking strange tongues; love and hate and all passions, heard and seen in music and laughter and cries, and agitated speech, and faces ashen white and burning red, and wide fixed eyes; tumults and wars upon wars, the shock of furious battle, the shouts of victory that frightened nature. And thereafter peace; toil and rest, and day and night; a young mother sitting on the summit of some high hill, looking out upon the vast range, the illimitable green world, the distant grey and silver sea, all the world sleeping in a peaceful sunshine and no cloud on all the sky; —a young mother fondling her firstborn and laughing in pure gladness of heart. And then the fading out of earth of that golden sunshine, and the grey chill evening of fear and flight; men drunk with blood, still thirsting for blood, their mouths frothing, their eyes ablaze, streaming over the hills, untiring as wolves on the track of the fugitives. The slayers in their turn are slain by death; in long quiet years there is a slow recovery of lost good, increase of people, and little children with shrill glad voices playing merry games in all the hollows of the hills, and staining their lips purple with blackberries, as in the old forgotten years. And once more strife, and all natural calamities— cold, and fever, and wasting famine; people with white skeleton faces sitting in rows on the hill-side, like those who sit by the river waiting for the slow ferryman to ferry them over, one by one. Slain by men or by some natural agency, still they pass and pass, and are succeeded by others—other tribes, other races, speaking a new language, but swayed by the same passion, and war still succeeds war. Then peace again, the lasting peace that causes all sweet and gentle feelings, all virtues, all graces, to flourish—the peace that is like a secret, unfelt malady which is slowly consuming a beautiful woman's life. And after long quiet, the battle-cry, the strange men with the old wolfish hunger and fury in their faces, the heavens darkened again with the smoke of cruel fires; and after the storm, quiet again, the old silence and desolation, wild-flowers blooming everywhere on the graves of a dead, forgotten people.

We can imagine that even he, albeit immortal, recalling and seeing again that immeasurable procession of human forms—the long long series of events and the millions of passionate, strenuous lives that have ceased to be—all compressed into a few moments of time, would feel his mind darkened with a sudden great shadow of sorrow. But the shadow would quickly pass; and his immortality would again be to him like the sun shining in a blue sky that is without a cloud.

Those who walk on the downs at this season, where they are highest and treeless, will sometimes feel that the loss of all that life and colour that made the summer so much to them is in some respects a gain. The vision that a little time ago roamed bee-like above the surface from bloom to bloom, ever finding and pausing to contemplate some fresh object of beauty or interest, is now free to take longer flights.

The sunlight may not be so bright, but the air is clearer now: there are mornings and whole days when the world is free from the haze that lately brooded on the scene and dimmed all things, when you can look beyond Sussex and see much of Kent and Surrey, Hampshire and the Isle of Wight. You may walk for a day along the hill-top, along the northern rim of the range, and seldom lose sight of the sea, its grey, immeasurable expanse silvered with the sunlight; while far down at your feet you have the flat wooded district of the weald. On its plain you see scattered village church towers and spires, and houses showing red, white, or slate-black among the green oaks; but the trees are everywhere so abundant in hedgerows and shaws and fragments of forest that it becomes easy mentally to see this region as it was before the Sussex iron workers so greatly altered it. One needs but to gaze on the scene, then close the eyes, and the gaps and the straight lines of hedge and fence, and the white and red spots of walls and roofs, and white puff of steam swiftly vanish, swallowed up or blotted out in the boundless expanse of deep uniform green, the unbroken forest of Andredsweald, as the Saxons and the Romans before them saw it from their encampments on the downs, and as William Hay, of Glyndbourne, described it a century ago in his *Mount Caburn*:

All was one wild inhospitable waste,
 Uncouth and horrid, desert and untraced.
 Hid by rough thickets from the face of day.
 The solitary realms of beasts of prey;

too gloomy for the nightingale to sing there, and too wet and cold and dark for the heat—and light-loving adder to have a home in it.

The hills in this clear autumn weather, familiar as their forms are and often as we have walked on them, seem almost like a new region to the eye, known and yet novel; the preternatural distinctness and nearness of the heights around us produce the illusion that we ourselves have changed to something better and higher, and have a more piercing sight and greater power and swiftness. It is as if like Mercury we had wings on our heels, and are able to move with a freedom never before known. Thus, in September, I at length begin to see men cantering over the open turfy downs without envying them their horses: at last the old second horse-back nature that clings to me drops off; the rider may gallop proudly past me to vanish over the next hill, yet leave me content and even glad to be on foot.

These walks on the downs in the cooler season are most exhilarating on the high, treeless, and in most places uncultivated hills east of the Adur. But for beautiful and varied scenery and abundance and variety of wild life, the range west of the Adur is most attractive in September and October, when the foliage, especially the beech, takes its autumn colour, and birds in thousands come down from the north to spend the winter, or remain for a short time in this district before crossing the sea.

CHAPTER XII

WEST OF THE ADUR

Autumn on the west downs—Abundance of birds—Village of Cocking—Drayton's *Polyolbion*—A company of magpies: their inconsequent behaviour—Magpie and domestic pigeon—Story of a pet magpie—Blackberries on the downs—Elderberries—Yews at Kingly Bottom—A tradition—Yew-berries and the missel-thrushes' orgy—Hawthorn wood—Charm of the thorn-tree—Beeches on the west downs—Effect of trees on the South Downs—Gilpin's strictures answered—Characteristic trees and bushes—Juniper—A curious effect—Character of the juniper-tree.

Throughout the southern half of England generally, the season from the beginning of April to the end of June is incomparably the most interesting time of the year to the bird lover. It is the season of the return of the migrants, of song, and of breeding. If there is a district which may be regarded as an exception it is assuredly that part of the Sussex downs west of the Adur, or perhaps it would be safer to say west of the Arun; for while the inland bird life in other places is diminishing day by day, here it is increasing. To these wooded and partially cultivated downs, and to the sheltered strip of rich, flat, maritime country that lies between them and the sea, birds in numbers resort in the autumn from the colder northern country, either to winter or to remain for some weeks or even months before crossing the sea. From September until November this movement and ingathering is going on, until the birds, visitors and residents, are incredibly abundant and a wonder to see. This abundance has been specially noticeable during the last three or four seasons, on account of the great increase in bird life throughout the country since the winter of 1894-5. Since that disastrous time there have been no killing frosts, and the summers have been favourable for breeding, with the result that our common small birds have increased and multiplied to an extraordinary extent. The increase is not, however, confined to the small passerines; it has been equally great in the rooks and wood-pigeons, and, in a less degree, in numerous other species.

One bright day in early October, at Cocking, I witnessed a pretty and amusing little comedy in bird life, which I relate not only for the interest of the incident but also to give an idea of the abundance of resident birds in this part of downland.

Cocking is one of many singularly interesting villages that nestle, half-hidden, in the shelter of the downs on the northern edge of the range. Out of a wooded combe in the side of the sheltering hill issues a stream, and where it flows or trickles past the village it spreads out and forms a marsh grown over with tall reed and flowering rush, in summer blue with water forget-me-not and water-mint. At the side of this blossoming marsh, in the middle of the green churchyard, sheltered and concealed by ancient trees, stands the small old church, one of the prettiest to be seen in the district. The stream is a part of the West Rother, that same pretty little river which Michael Drayton some three centuries ago spoke of as running wild in the woods where it, or she, lived, and being no comfort to the aged hill who was her father. Drayton was all for personifying the principal features in the landscape—hills, valleys, woods, marshes, rivers, and what not. Male and female made he them, and of all ages, connected with each other by human ties of all kinds; and when he gets into a broken country like this it becomes difficult to follow him, and to know what the pother is all about; for his characters are always quarrelling among themselves and threatening in lofty rhymes to "do" for each other.

Going to the top of the hill above Cocking I sat down against a hedge, which sheltered me from the wind, and looked upon the scene spread out before me. At the foot of the bare down ran a low thorn hedge, dividing it from the yellow stubble fields beyond. At each end of the hedge there were masses of high trees, fir and beech, and among the trees on one side a farm-house and buildings were seen. Beyond the bare down and fields and village, the flat, wooded district of the weald spread out before me, with the little red-coloured town of Midhurst in the middle of the picture. As I sat there, idly watching the wood-pigeons constantly arriving in small parties of three or four to a dozen to settle down on the yellow stubble field beneath me, then letting my sight rest on the small red town two or three miles away, and, a mile or so to the west of it, the village and station of Elstead, it all at once came into my mind that close by, in the small village of Trotton, where his father was curate, Otway was born. Taking up my binocular, I began excitedly seeking among the green oaks near Elstead for that famous spot, but before I could satisfy myself that I had picked it out a chance glance at the yellow field at the foot of the down revealed a black and white patch on the pale stubble which had not been there a few minutes before. Bringing my glasses to bear on the patch, which was alive and moving, I discovered that it was a party of fifteen magpies busily running about feeding and playfully chasing one another on the ground. This was to me a most astonishing sight; it is rare in England to see as many as fifteen magpies together, even where game is not preserved, and here I was in a corner of Sussex where pheasant-preserving is carried to an extreme that occasionally excites the disgust of even the most enthusiastic sportsmen. Not far from the spot where I was sitting there was one small property which was notoriously overstocked with pheasants, and yet because a big man was coming down for one day's shooting, the owner, not satisfied that his birds would be enough, had just bought five hundred more and put them in his woods. They were thicker on the ground than fowls on a poultry-farm, and tamer than fowls.

Naturally, after catching sight of these miraculous magpies, I thought no more about unhappy Otway, but gave all my attention to them, and counted them at least fifteen times over to make sure that they were fifteen. Not many yards from them, near the low hedge, a number of pheasants were sunning themselves; and by the side of the flock of magpies a covey of nine or ten partridges were slowly and quietly moving about, searching for grain; and all about them and over the whole field of many acres the wood-pigeons in twos and threes and larger parties were also quietly feeding, while fresh parties were continually arriving. In that clear air and bright sunshine they looked lavender-coloured on the pale yellow stubble. The wood-pigeons scattered over the field must have numbered six or seven hundred. It was curious and amusing to note the behaviour of the magpies, flighty, inconsequent, and perpetually interfering with one another, when thus seen side by side with the diligent, quietly-moving pigeons and partridges, each occupied with his own business. One magpie would find or pretend to find something which he would look down at very intently, and at once two or three of his neighbours would rush excitedly up; then all of them, putting their heads together, would stare at the strange object for a few seconds, and then fall to quarrelling, or chasing each other's long tails round and round, or doing some other ridiculous thing.

By-and-by a domestic pigeon, a pretty red bird with conspicuous white wing-feathers, came flying from the farm-house not far off and settled down to feed among some wood-pigeons, twenty or thirty yards from the magpies. One of the magpies raised its head and gazed intently for some moments at the new-comer, then rising rushed at and drove it away with violence. The pigeon circled over the field two or three times, then alighted again a little further away. Again the same magpie got up and went for it; and the same thing happened over and over again, until the persecuted pigeon gave up trying to feed there and flew back to the farm-house, and the magpie, well satisfied, returned to its game of romps with its fellows. How amusing these crow-brained creatures are, not only when we see them as pets, and laugh at their pranks, but away from us in their wild state where there is no human witness of their actions! They are like preternaturally shrewd and mischief-loving little boys, who for the love of wildness in them have been changed into wild birds. I could imagine this particular magpie saying, "No, no! You may be a very pretty bird, and inoffensive, and a first cousin of our friend and neighbour the ringdove, who lays very nice eggs in summer; but you are tame, domestic, and have no business to come here to associate with wild birds. Off you go! " That evening, at the inn where I was staying, I spoke about the magpies and their funny little ways, my mind being still full of the subject, whereupon the landlady told me the following story. Her husband, she said, was exceedingly fond of magpies, and always kept one when he had the chance, and this fondness dated back to the period of childhood, when a very amusing tame magpie was kept by his father. He was a carpenter in a little rustic village in North Hampshire; his earnings were small, and he was accustomed to hand over a sum of twenty shillings to his wife every Saturday for housekeeping. There were nine children to keep, and to make the most of her money she used to go on Saturday afternoon to the nearest town, six miles distant, to purchase the week's provisions and groceries and anything else that was required. Two or three of the biggest children would accompany her to help her with the basket on their return. Now it fell out that on a certain Saturday she had all her money in one coin, a gold sovereign, and this she placed on the kitchen dresser while putting her things on; but in a few minutes, when she was ready to start, the money was gone. Naturally the whole house was thrown into the greatest trouble and excitement, and immediately everyone began hunting in every likely and unlikely place for the missing sovereign, for now the poor distracted woman began to think that she could not have put it on the dresser after all. But it could not be found, and when hope was gone she could not restrain her tears; and the children, seeing her crying, realised that there would be no exciting visit to the town, no Saturday afternoon sweeties, nor any good things in the house, but a long, long week of want before them, and they too burst out crying. It was then that the eldest girl all at once thought of the pet magpie they kept, and of its love of mischief; and, jumping up, she ran to the open cage which served the bird as a roosting-place by night, and which he occasionally visited by day. And there the coin was found, stuck edgeways between the wooden floor and side of the cage, and in a moment, at a loud cry of joy from the finder, the tears and lamentations of the whole house were turned to laughter and happiness.

There is an abundance of wild fruit to attract fruit-eating birds to the downs in autumn. Throughout the range, including the high treeless South Downs, the bramble flourishes greatly among the furze on the slopes, and in the combes and valleys; and from July to the end of September the bushes are covered with clusters of the beautiful blue-black and crimson embossed berries for every hand and beak to pluck. The hands are few indeed except in the vicinity of Brighton—a pleasant place "for a Wen, " as Cobbett said of it, but too populous now, and no longer pleasant to those who love to look upon an unsullied nature. On a blazing August day I have seen two miles of dusty road running inland from the town sprinkled with a straggling procession of poor children, many of them too small and feeble for such an adventure—children from the slums and mean streets of the overgrown Islington-by-the-Sea; a long straggling column of ragamuffins out on a raiding expedition to the distant brambly downs, each carrying a bag, or basket, or mug, or tin pail, or old tea-kettle, or some other kitchen utensil, in which to store the juicy loot. Away from Brighton, outside of its smoke-cloud, and out of sight of its people, big and little, creeping like black ants over the green hills, the wild garden is all for the birds. They are many, and they feast every day and all day long; but for all their feasting the fruit is still plentiful when, in early October, the devil flies abroad, as some believe, to spit on the bramble-bushes and make its berries uneatable.

The elder is common on the downs, and ripens early, and I have noticed that the berries are devoured as fast as they ripen; not, I think, because they taste better than blackberries to the birds, but because they are so easily gathered, and being small and round, are easily swallowed whole even by the smallest bird. A bird, as a rule, likes to swallow his fruit rather than to peck at it; he generally has to peck at the blackberry, and, compared with the clusters of the elderberry, it is not so easily got at.

Of our fruit-eating birds the missel-thrush is the most common on the downs; this bird loves the yew-berry above all wild fruits, and there is one spot in this district where he can feast on it as he cannot do anywhere else in the kingdom. This is at the famous "grove, " as it is called, of yews at Kingly Bottom, in one of the prettiest spots among the West Sussex downs, near the small village of West Stoke, about five miles from Chichester. The grove is an isolated wood, or rather forest, composed almost wholly of yew trees, growing in a broad combe in the side of a down; and above the dark green of the yews the round light-green summit is seen like a head crowned with a row of immense barrows. Tradition tells that at this spot a great battle was fought by the men of Chichester against the Danes about eleven centuries ago, and that the slain sea-kings were buried in the mounds on the hill, hence the name of Kingly Vale or Bottom. The belief is that many of these yew trees are two thousand years old. In one part of the wood, on the right hand as you go up from the vale, there is no undergrowth, and in this part you may walk freely among the dark religious trees with trunks like huge rudely-fashioned pillars of red and purple ironstone. One has here the sensation of being in a vast cathedral; not like that of Chichester, but older and infinitely vaster, fuller of light and gloom and mystery, and more wonderful in its associations. Coming from this sacred dim interior, I have found on its threshold a tree the like of which is hardly to be seen in England. This is a large and very perfect yew with horizontal branches of great length, the lowest of which come down to the ground on all sides, and are interwoven with and form part of an immense and most beautiful tangle of juniper, thorn, bramble and briar, grown through and overgrown and bound together with honeysuckle and deep green ivy and light green traveller's joy, the last hoary-silver with its profusion of downy dry seed-feathers. I had measured the trunks of other trees, but the girth of this could not be taken unless a man went down on his belly and drew himself snakewise through the protecting natural hedge. May no sacrilegious hand with hatchet or billhook ever cut a way through it.

This wood is a paradise of the missel-thrushes in autumn. Numerous all over the downs, it is not strange when rough weather comes that they should gather to it, not only for the sake of the perfect shelter from the rain and wind it affords, but also for the abundance of the fruit they like so well. They seem to delight as much in its insipid sweet taste as in the somewhat acrid flavour of the orange-scarlet rowan-berries. In the yew-berry there is a disagreeable bitterness under the sweet gummy pulp, which is probably deleterious in a slight degree; but the bird tastes only the sweet, and is not concerned about the wholesomeness of his food when he is eating not to satisfy hunger, but purely for pleasure. In most places where yew trees are few and far between, we see that the missel-thrushes, assisted by the song-thrush and blackbird, devour the fruit as soon as it ripens. In this wood the profusion is so great that the birds can go on with their feast into October without making much impression on the myriads of rose-coloured berries that gem the dark feathery foliage. And they do feast! It is worse than a feast, it is a perfect orgy. When a bird, with incredible greediness, has gorged to repletion he flies down to a spot where there is a nice green turf and disgorges, then, relieved, he goes back with a light heart to gorge again, and then again. The result is that every patch or strip of green turf among or near the trees is thickly sprinkled over with little masses or blobs of disgorged fruit, bright pinky red in colour, looking like strawberries scattered about the ground and crushed by passing feet, In a single blob or pellet I have counted as many as twenty-three whole berries, as bright red as when on the tree, embedded in a mass of viscid pulp, mixed with many of the dark green and poisonous stones of the half-digested berries.

The wood I have described, where the intemperate missel-thrushes have their revels, is almost unique in character: there is on the downs west of the Adur another wood of a kind rarely seen that has a singular charm. This is a hawthorn wood growing on the high downs east of the village of Findon, and about halfway between Cissbury Hill and Chancton-bury Ring. I have come across patches of wood, exclusively thorns, in Savernake Forest, Albury Park, and on private estates in different parts of the country, but not one comparable to this in extent and beauty. The peculiar charm of the hawthorn—and that it possesses a very great charm everyone will allow—appears to be due to its variety—to the individuality as well as the beauty of the tree. It certainly has a specific character as marked as that of any forest tree we have, and is quite unlike any other, unless we say that it is a miniature oak in appearance, and has the attractive roughness and majesty of the great tree in little, with a more varied and tender colour, more light and shade, a richer beauty. This is the specific character: then there is the very piquant individual character, which is an added distinction; for two thorns are not like two oaks, or beeches, or elms. Many forest trees are best seen in masses; for instance, the elm in its summer foliage and the beech in its autumn colour. The hawthorn, like the holly and, in a less degree, some other trees, is best seen growing by itself; and the most perfect thorn wood is that where there is ample room for a person to walk freely about in it and see every tree, or a large proportion of the trees, all round. That is the character of the wood I am describing, and its beauty is greatly enhanced by the character of the open sunlit ground it grows on—a soft elastic turf, like that of the sheep-walks, but more closely eaten down by the innumerable rabbits that have their home in the wood; its harmonious greens and browns touched or mixed with the brighter colours of lichen and moss, rust-red and orange and tender grey and emerald-green.

Here, better than in most places, the infinite variety of the thorn may be admired, especially in its colour, from August onward to October, when the many-tinted leaves are finally shed. It is a familiar fact that the drier and poorer the soil on which a tree grows the more beautiful will be the dying colours of the foliage; and these thorns on the high chalk hills are doubtless more brilliantly coloured in September than most trees of their kind. But though so various and charming on that account, you do not get masses of splendid colour in the thorn, owing to the looseness of its foliage and to the various colours and shades of colour which may be seen on almost any tree. Or if in any one tree you get a mass of intense colour, it is in the fruit and not the leaf. Here are many trees so entirely covered with berries as to appear at a short distance like trees cut out of deepest crimson coral.

For great masses of intense colour nothing can compare with the beech, which flourishes above all trees on the West Sussex downs. And here it may be remarked that it is not only in its magnificent autumn colours that the beech adds greatly to the attractiveness of the downland scenery in West Sussex. At other seasons, too, even when stript bare, the tall beeches please the eye. One would say that it was a very bold experiment to plant groves of beeches and firs on the summits of these round, smooth, pale green hills, yet it has been justified by the fine effect produced. Here are groves that remind one of the unrivalled Hollywater Clump in Wolmer Forest—groves visible at an immense distance, standing like many-pillared temples on the high hills. One does not wish even these most conspicuous groves away, because, I imagine, the country is wooded generally, and the hills are more scattered about and not so high; it is a broken wooded country, and the tall, slender beeches and firs predominate.

On the South Downs proper, east of the Adur, the case is wholly different: the hills are larger and there is less tillage; the clumps or groves and woods so few that the effect is strange and inharmonious. The isolated grove that springs suddenly to the sight as one mounts a hill, shady and deepest green on a pale unshaded country, is a blot on the landscape; and here, if anywhere in England, one would be glad to see an axe laid at the root of trees of noble growth. For one cannot say of these trees that they are the "nobler growth of thought, " rather we might say that in planting trees in such a place we have been playing fantastic tricks with nature.

I must confess that I am speaking only for myself; perhaps no one would agree with me; and it may be that many a pilgrim to the South Downs, who has cooled himself in burning summer weather in the delicious shade of Stanmer, will consider my words almost sacrilegious. Then I have to reckon with Parson Gilpin, who rode over these downs a century or longer ago, and scornfully said of them that they were "entirely destitute of ornament. " An occasional glimpse of the sea, he wrote, imparted a little life and variety to the tame monotonous scene. It is true that he gave a little faint praise to the situation of Lewes; but even this he qualified by saying that the hills round Lewes were chalk—"and chalk spoils any landscape. " Poor old chalk!

I am not abusing Gilpin; on the contrary, I love and reverence his memory because of his life-work, about which he wrote no book, and told the world nothing. Nevertheless, I cannot help smiling when I recall the fact that this last book, in which, like the glorified landscape gardener that he was, he spoke in disprise of the downs, was inscribed *to the memory* of a still living wife, the faithful companion of his rambles for over fifty years. Of course he quite expected that she would be gone before the book was out; but he was greatly mistaken, just like the rogues who lied in the famous ballad of the mad dog and the man who was bitten by it. He it was, even Gilpin, who died, leaving his good wife alive and well to publish the book, dedication and all!

One need not fear to offend the parson of Boldre by poking a little fun at him at this distant day, so long after he visited Sussex and spoke slightingly of chalk. His subsequent rambles, of which we have no report, must have considerably enlarged his ideas about scenery and other matters.

We have seen that the West Sussex downs excel in the beauty of their beeches; that they can boast of the noblest grove or wood of yew trees in this country, and also possess a hawthorn wood of rare beauty. It may be added that the furze also flourishes at numerous points from end to end of the range: many and many a shining yellow sheet of bloom, from three or four to twenty or thirty acres in extent, have I seen and revelled in among these hills in May and June. Here, too, that charming climber, the wild clematis or traveller's joy, finds its most favourable soil, and flourishes amazingly. I have never seen it look so fine in winter as among the downs; in sheltered hollows among the hills you will find clumps of trees, evergreen holly and yew, mixed with leafless oak and thorn and beech, partially veiled or clouded with the unshed silver-grey fluff to a height of thirty or forty feet from the ground. In England we call that silver-grey down *Old Man's Beard*; in another country I have heard it called *Angel's Hair*.

There is another fine plant characteristic of the Sussex downs, the jumper, which is not flourishing; and this is all the more to be regretted, because it is not, like the furze and thorn and clematis, to be found all over the land; compared with these species the juniper is a rare plant, very local in its distribution. In many places the ground has been cleared of it to give better food to the sheep, or when well grown it has been cut down for fuel and for other purposes; and we may say that in many places the juniper is disappearing from the downs simply because the great landowners have not thought proper to preserve it. Yet how congenial the soil is to it, how readily it grows, may be seen on some downs, as at Kingly Vale for instance, where large areas are covered or rather thickly sprinkled over with its bushes. But you will not find here one large or well-grown bush; it is all a dwarf scrub, where no doubt the largest plants are periodically cut down.

One must go to other districts, in many cases where the soil is less favourable to it, but where it has not been ill-treated, to see the juniper in its perfection. It is a handsome plant, but its greatest attraction lies in its variety. The variety of the hawthorn, which gives a charm to that tree, consists as much in colour and light and shadow as in form; in the juniper the variety is in the form rather than in colour. To appreciate this character of the plant, it must be seen where it is pretty abundant, on some open spot away from all other tree and bush vegetation. At a distance it may be mistaken for a furze-bush, being not unlike that plant in size, colour, and manner of growth. Seen nearer, it is not of so rough and prickly an aspect; its pine-needle-like fine foliage give it a somewhat feathery appearance; it is brighter green than the furze; the topmost slender sprays, gracefully curved at their tips, are tinged with red; and where the foliage is thick there is a bluish tint on the green that is like a bloom. In some lights, especially in the early mornings, when the level sunbeams strike on the bushes, wet with dew or melting hoar-frost, this blueness gives the plant a rare, delicate, changeful beauty. Even here on the downs, where most of the junipers one finds are a poor scrub, I have been enchanted at the effects produced by the light on it, but the loveliest effect was in part fortuitous, and came as a delightful surprise.

The south-west gales of October and November had blown the fallen leaves of a beech-wood for miles over the downs, and at one spot where an area of thirty or forty acres was thickly sprinkled over with a juniper scrub, a drift of yellow and red leaves had formed at the foot of every bush. Here, on the light green smooth turf, the little bushes or tufts, three or four feet apart, showing a blue bloom and play of rainbow colour in their feathery green foliage, each with its drift of intense russet-gold at its foot, made a very singular and very beautiful picture.

Where the juniper is abundant and grows large, the plants are curiously unlike, and, viewed at a distance of a couple of hundred yards or so, they have something of the appearance of a grove or wood of miniature trees of different species: alike in colour, in their various forms they look some like isolated clumps of elms, others columnar in shape, others dome-like, resembling evergreen oaks or well-grown yews; and among these and many other forms there are tall straight bushes resembling Lombardy poplars and pointed cypresses.

It is, however, not often that one may see even the large fine junipers all *shapely* in their various forms: some are ragged unlovely bushes, and this is most often the case where they grow in woods and are to some extent shaded by other trees.

It is to be wished that something could be done to prevent the destruction of this handsome bush. If some one of the great landowners of the downs would but create a juniper preserve at some point where the plant grows spontaneously and well, he would deserve the gratitude of all lovers of nature who are accustomed to take their summer rambles in downland.

CHAPTER XIII

THE MARITIME DISTRICT

The autumnal movement of birds—Linnets on the downs—
Birds wintering in the maritime district—Character of the
district—Birdham—Rooks and starlings—Skylarks and
finches—Dun-nock and wren—Pewits on the Cuckmere—
Pewit's hatred of the rook—Pewit's wing-exercises—Pewits
in flocks—Black-headed gulls—Charm of the maritime
district—Gloomy weather—Missel-thrush: his temper,
habits, and song—The spire of Chichester Cathedral: its
aesthetic value in the landscape.

The autumnal movement of birds, both migrants and residents, is
most marked throughout the downland and maritime districts of
Sussex during the month of October. Swallows gather in numbers in
the weald at the foot of the downs, but on the long strip of country,
hilly and flat, that lies between the weald district and the sea the
insectivorous migrants are not much seen, as they do not break their
journey here. The exceptions are the wheatear, pied wagtail,
stonechat (travelling in small flocks), and the meadow-pipit. In
October, when cold and wet weather has set the more dilatory seed-
eating migrants in motion, together with all those kinds that leave
their summer haunts to winter elsewhere within the country, birds
in multitudes arrive at this "threshold of England, " some to rest and
recruit their strength before taking their flight across the Channel,
others in search of suitable winter quarters; and so long as the
weather permits, numbers of these travellers keep to the hills.

On the cultivated downland farms the linnets are most abundant,
and if the weather keeps mild, will haunt the stubble-fields down to
the end of November. As many as three or four thousand birds may
sometimes be seen in a flock, and it is a fine spectacle when they rise
and wheel about the field, and after three or four turns drop down, a
shower of birds, vanishing all at once from sight. A person may then
stand within fifty yards of the flock without hearing the faintest
sound, or being able to see one of the little brown creatures busily
searching for seeds on the brown soil; then suddenly they are all up
again, an innumerable multitude of swiftly-rushing twittering
birdlings, brought, as it were, by a miracle into existence!

From the stubbles they fly to a brake or thick hedge, and sit so closely crowded together on every twig that the leafless thorns are brown with them on the sunny side. If the weather be not too cold one may then hear the winter singing of the linnet, delightful to listen to. Heard at a distance of sixty or seventy yards, it is like the rushing sound the wind makes in beechen woods in summer; but when the listener goes nearer he finds that this confused noise is composed of innumerable fine melodious notes, a mass and an indescribable tangle of sound, resembling the evening concert of an immense host of starlings, gathered at their roosting-place, but more musical.

These large flocks are probably made up of birds from hundreds of furze-grown commons, moors, and mountain-sides all over the kingdom, and will by-and-by take their departure to countries beyond the sea. When cold blasts have driven these and all other loiterers from the exposed hills, the maritime district is then the chief haunt and winter home of birds. Probably this district has the most numerous and varied feathered population to be found anywhere in England during the winter months.

The strip of low country extending along the coast from the mouth of the river Adur to the border of Hampshire has a strongly-marked character of its own. The extreme fertility of the soil, and the mildness of the climate, due to the shelter of the downs on the north side, and to the nearness of the sea, which is never cold, has made Worthing what it is—the chief vineyard and garden of rare fruits in England. This is the character of the maritime district, although where the range of hills retires furthest from the sea, the flat country is less sheltered from the north and east winds. But throughout the climate is remarkably mild, even in the widest part between the downs and the promontory of Selsey Bill. In January, after walking from Harting over downs white with half-frozen snow, when a furious north-east wind was blowing, I came to Selsey, and found a different climate. There was no snow on the green fields and muddy roads; the wind was light and not unpleasantly cold, and thrushes, hedge-sparrows, and wrens were singing.

A few miles from Chichester, on an arm of the sea, which at low water is mostly a mud-flat, there is a parish and village of Birdham, or Bridham. This birds' home doubtless acquired its name in early Saxon times, on account of the great numbers of sea—and water-fowl that resorted to the spot in winter; and Chichester harbour is still a favourite haunt of water-fowl in severe weather. But the entire maritime district is a Birdham in winter: the mild climate, everlasting verdure, abundance of food and water, and a sparse human population make it indeed an ideal wintering-place for many birds that have their breeding haunts on the hills and other exposed districts throughout the country.

Rooks and starlings are excessively abundant. It is a wonder how any grub can escape their prying eyes and busy prodding beaks. On some favourite feeding-grounds the surface is often covered with grass and moss plucked up by them to get at the grubs at the roots. When the grass freshly pulled up is examined, the leaves are invariably seen to be wilted or of a sickly colour. It is indeed this faded appearance of the grass that reveals the hiding-place of the larva to the bird, and it may be safely said that he never pulls a blade of grass without sufficient reason. But the starlings pull up moss in most places on the chance, I imagine, of finding insects concealed under it. Skylarks winter on the grassy flats in considerable numbers, and flocks of bramb-lings are met with everywhere. Flocks, too, of chaffinches, yellowhammers, corn and reed buntings, and linnets and redpolls. But the goldfinches are a very few solitary birds: you will see perhaps two or three in a day's walk, and you will probably see quite as many grey wagtails, or even kingfishers. One day in the course of an eight miles' walk I saw two rare birds—one goldfinch and one great crested grebe.

I have said in a former chapter that the dunnock, or hedge-sparrow, breeds in the furze-bushes all over the downs, but in the cold season forsakes that part of the country. Doubtless many of those downland birds spend the winter in the maritime district, where they are extremely numerous in December and January. The downland wrens may have the same habits, as they are just as abundant: as you walk the brisk little brown bird flits out of the scanty hedges or from the sides of the ditches at every few yards.

Herons come to fish, and pewits are common, but not in such great numbers as we often see them in the valleys of the rivers Arun, Ouse, and Cuck-mere. The artist's picture of the narrow valley of the last-named stream, taken from a point close to Exceat Bridge, on a November evening, shows a large flock of these birds that continued flying near us and passing and repassing over our heads during the whole time he was occupied in making the sketch.

The pewit breeds in all the downland valleys, and I have often amused myself watching him defending the field where he had his nest against all suspected birds. When the hills are dry in summer the moist green fields and water-meadows are attractive to the downland rooks; but these white-faced crows are hated by the plover, and he will not allow them to feed on the sacred ground where his treasures are. The rook, we know, is an egg-stealer on occasion; the pewit evidently believes that he is always one, and he perhaps knows him better than we do. Still, it is rather hard on the hungry rook; for it may happen that the meadow or field forbidden to him is precisely the one which he is most anxious to investigate. Hundreds of starlings, those lesser rooks he is accustomed to associate with, may be there, full in sight, feasting on fat grubs; but no sooner does he come to join them than the jealous pewit is up in arms, and then begins that furious persecution which he cannot stand against, and flying from it he is chased and buffeted for a distance of five or six hundred yards from the ground.

In September and October the resident pewits are joined by others of their kind; and in the valley of the Cuckmere, a favourite wintering-ground, you may see a flock of as many as two thousand birds, looking at a distance, when they are up and flying round, like a vast cloud of starlings. No bird appears to take greater pleasure in the exercise of his own powers of flight than the pewit. Flying is to him like riding, cycling, rowing or sailing, and skating (I wish I could add ballooning or rushing about in a flying-machine) to ourselves. It is his sport; and during the spring and summer season, when pewits live in pairs or small parties, he spends a great part of his time in those quite useless, but doubtless exhilarating, displays which we are never tired of watching. Rising to a considerable height in the air, he lets himself go, with the determination apparently of breaking the pewit record; that is to say, of rushing downwards in the approved suicidally insane manner, with sudden doublings this way and that, and other violent eccentric motions designed to make him lose his head; and finally to come at fullest speed within an inch, or as much less than an inch as he can, of dashing himself into a pulp on the ground below.

Blake, in his tiger song, exclaims:

And what shoulder, and what art,
Could twist the sinews of thy heart?

The pewit, too, compared with man, must have a remarkable heart, and brain, and nerves, to do such things purely for the fun of it. Here, sitting on a hill-side, I watched a male bird, amusing himself in the air while his mate was on the nest, rise up and repeat the action of pretending to go mad and hurl himself down to destruction over fifty times without resting. Then he alighted, and I began to imagine what his sensations must be: his brain, I thought, must seem to him to have got away somehow from his body and to be rushing madly this way and that through the air. Meantime the bird was standing placidly regarding his mate; then he nodded his head once or twice to her, and in a twinkling was off, high up, and at his capers once more.

In autumn and winter, when a large number of pewits are congregated, their wing-exercises are mostly of another kind. Each bird is then, like the starling, or linnet, or dunlin, in its flock, one of a company; and we see and note not individuals but an entire crowd, or army, moved by one mind or impulse. The birds often spend many hours of the day in the air, travelling up and down stream, often changing their formation; now seen as a flock, a mass, extending wings on either side, until they present a front of several hundred feet in length, then closing again and changing their disposition they are seen as a long column or winding stream of birds. The smoothness and discipline with which these evolutions are conducted incline one to think that sight and hearing in some gregarious species of aerial habits are supplemented by another faculty—a very delicate sense of touch, as in the bat; that it is a sensation of repulsion informing each member of the flock of the nearness to it of others, and prevents them from touching or striking against and impeding one another. When the flock turns or changes its formation, it may be observed that while numbers of birds are streaming away to this or that side with accelerated speed, others, at points where confusion would seem inevitable, suspend their flight, and remain almost motionless at equal distances apart until the moment comes for them to join in the swift movement.

Black-headed gulls are as abundant as rooks on the flat country and on the neighbouring downs where there is tillage, and may often be seen in screaming crowds following close at the heels of the ploughman. When not feeding they are seen at rest on a green field, and at a distance may be taken for a great patch of unmelted snow. That beautiful order which so many gregarious birds observe when on the wing in flocks is adhered to by the gulls even when resting on the earth. They invariably sit or stand on the grass with beaks all pointing one way, to the wind, all at equal distances apart. These white flocks resting on the green fields are a familiar feature of the winter landscape in this district.

Altogether, this is a spot in which an observer of wild birds may pass a very pleasant winter season. For others, too, the flat land with its mild climate and perpetual verdure must have a charm in spite of miry ways and sodden soil. Even under a grey sky, and it is not always grey, there is colour in the landscape. The trees are mostly elms, and their rich browns and purples relieve the universal green of the earth. Ivy is most luxuriant in this damp land, and wraps the trunks and branches of trees, and houses and fences, in its dark mantle. On account of the very limited horizon a man has when on a perfectly flat surface, the leaflessness of the winter trees is an advantage here, and enables one to see the distant small villages scattered over the district; the stone farm-house, its old red-tiled roof stained with many-coloured moss and lichen; the great barn and outbuildings, thatched with pale yellow straw; and the small, ancient, ivied Norman church, with the sacred yew in its churchyard. In late autumn, when the shortness and darkness of the days are most noticeable, and in winter, there are often long spells of mild, wet weather, when the south-west wind blows continuously, when it rains every day, until the green earth is like a swollen sponge, and the roads are deep with mire, and stream and ditch and drain are full to overflowing; when in the intervals of the rain and in rainless days there are driving mists, sudden showers, and everywhere the spray and smell of salt water and of seaweed. Days, too, without any rain, when the vast heavens are filled with clouds that have never a rift nor a sunlit spot in them; a universe of slaty-black vapour, miles deep, rising ever from the dim moaning sea to drown the earth and all that is in it in everlasting gloom. Such days are known all over the land and depress the soul, and when such a cloud has been long above us we pine for a sight of the pure blue of heaven and the sunshine, even as a prisoner pines for liberty.

Yet, strange as it may sound, this low, flat land on a level with the sea has had the greatest charm for me in precisely such gloomy weather as I have described. In summer this district does not attract me; I look at the hills and would be walking on their elastic turf, and breathing that exhilarating air. The summer atmosphere is heavy and motionless here; still, one would say that winter wet and gloom would make the place intolerable. I can only suppose that on account of the lowness and flatness of the land, the nearness of the sea and the superabundant moisture, the gloom is deepest here in dark weather—it has always seemed so to me; and that the darkness serves to accentuate the special character of the district, and pleases me for that reason. That my pleasure is as great as that which I experience on the treeless hills in July and August, when the sun is brightest, I do not for a moment say; I can only say that in the gloomiest weather, a perpetual twilight which made trees, buildings, hedges, cattle, and all objects look dim and distant even when close by, I have rambled all day long without any sense of depression or weariness; and that when, hungry and thirsty, I have sought refreshment at one of the little village inns, and have found only stale bread without any cheese to eat, and nothing but four-ale to drink—ale at fourpence a quart—I have eaten the bread and drunk the beer (a tankard, not a quart of it), and have gone forth comforted and happy to resume my wanderings.

There is one thing to make a lover of bird-music happy in the darkest weather in January in this maritime district. Mid-winter is the season of the missel-thrush. The song-thrush has been heard since the end of November, but he is not the true winter singer. He is heard often enough—a bird here and a bird there—when the sun shines, and in cloudy or in wet weather too, if it be mild. But when it is too gloomy for even his fine temper, when there is no gleam of light anywhere and no change in that darkness of immense ever-moving cloud above; and the south-west raves all day and all night, and day after day, then the storm-cock sings his loudest from a tree-top and has no rival. A glorious bird!

He breeds earlier than most birds, and we have seen that after that labour is ended he repairs to the downs and leads a gipsy existence in bands of a dozen or so, feeding on snails and grasshoppers, drinking at the dew-ponds, and resting at noon in the shade of the furze-bushes; also that in autumn he feasts (often too well) on wild fruits, especially the poisonous yew-berry. But during all that pleasant vagrant summer life, when he sings not and has no family cares, he is still in disposition the bird we know so well in the orchard and copse, the big olive-coloured spotty thrush that sits motionless and statuesque and flies from you with an angry scream; the bird whose courageous spirit and fierce onslaught in defence of his nest makes him the equal of crafty crows and pies, and of hawks, in spite of their hooked beaks and cruel sharp talons. Those large black conspicuous spots on his breast and his habit of singing in weather that makes all other voices silent, seem appropriate to a bird of his bold aggressive temper.

As I walked one hot day on the northern ridge of the South Downs, a party of half a dozen missel-thrushes flew up from the ground before me, and rising high in the air went away towards the weald. A telegraph line crosses the hills at that point, and just when the thrushes rose up and flew from me a sparrow-hawk came up swiftly flying over the ridge and perched on the telegraph wire. I have observed that this hawk, like the cuckoo, cannot properly grasp the wire and sit firm and upright on it as most passerine birds are able to do. Like the cuckoo he wobbles and drops his wings upon the wire to help to keep him up. It was so in the present case: the hawk was swaying about trying to hold on to the thin smooth wire when the thrushes passed over him, thirty or forty yards above, all but one, and this one remained hovering motionless in the air for a space of a few seconds directly above the hawk, then dropped like a stone upon his back, and knocked him clean off his perch.

It is often stated by writers on British birds that the missel-thrush ceases singing in March or April; this is a mistake, as I frequently hear him in May and June. But why, I have often asked myself, is he silent on many days in January and February when the weather is mild, and the song-thrush is loudest? I have a suspicion that the missel-thrush is less tolerant of other bird-voices near him than most species; and I think that the loud persistent singing of the song-thrush is more disturbing to him than any other bird-voice. At all events, I have often listened for the missel-thrush, in localities where he was abundant, and have not heard him when the song-thrush was singing. In the same localities I have heard the missel-thrush singing everywhere on days when his rival was silent.

When all the most luscious of the wild fruits have been eaten, and frosts and winds make the open downs impossible to live on, the missel-thrushes break up their flocks and every bird goes back to his lowland home. There is then not an orchard, nor copse, nor grove, without a pair of the big thrushes; and on the flat-wooded country on the north of the downs these birds are, I think, just as numerous. Home again from his long outing, the missel-thrush soon begins to sing; and if you should observe him in rough or gloomy weather, perched on an elm-top, swayed about this way and that by the gusts, singing his best, you must believe that this dark aspect of things delights him; that his pleasure in life, expressed with such sounds and in such circumstances, must greatly exceed in degree the contentment and bliss that is ours, even when we are most free from pain or care, and our whole beings most perfectly in tune with nature.

As to the song; although we probably value it most for its associations, and because it is often heard when other bird-voices are silent, it is also beautiful in itself. The sound is beautiful in quality, but the singer has no art, and flings out his notes anyhow; the song is an outburst, a cry of happiness, and is over in a moment, and after a moment of silence he repeats it, and so on for ten or twenty minutes or longer. In its quality the sound is most like the blackbird's; and when, in early spring, the blackbird, perched on a tree-top, first tries his long-disused voice, the short confused phrases he blurts out are so like the song of the missel-thrush that anyone may be easily deceived by them. The difference in the voices of the two birds is that the missel-thrush is not so full and mellow, and is slightly metallic or bell-like; and it is probably due to this quality that the song carries much further than that of the blackbird.

What the missel-thrush is to the hearing, the spire of Chichester Cathedral is to the sight in this flat district—the chief feature and object of beauty and interest for the eyes to rest upon. In a way it is always present. It may be seen at an immense distance from the downs—from Cissbury Hill, for instance, and from the hill-tops far away to the west, and from the borders of Hampshire; but down on the flat green country amidst which it rises, so tall and lessening to a point, we look at it with different eyes, and its aesthetic value in the scene is greater and of a different kind.

The sound, too, of the cathedral bell, booming out the hour in deep, measured strokes, will, if the wind be favourable, follow you many a mile as you walk by the harbour—

Over the wide-watered shore
Swinging slow with sullen roar.

Where Milton heard the great bell he had in his mind when he wrote the lines in Penseroso I do not know, but they admirably describe this great bell sound from the vast bell-tower at Chichester, when it travels seawards over the flat harbour country, where land and water mix. It is the character of the country, its flatness and silence and the loneliness of its shores, that gives to this one great sound its importance, or value. For a similar reason this solitary soaring spire has a value above that of any other spire in the land.

We are accustomed to hear Salisbury Cathedral greatly praised; and as a spire it is doubtless very great, a more beautiful and a nobler work than that of Chichester. There is no comparison. Nevertheless, I admire Chichester most, in spite of its inferiority when viewed merely as a work of art. But I do not look at it with the architect's eye. In the inferior work I see nothing but an object that fits in with and forms a part of the landscape: more than that, it "pulls" the scene together, and gives it a unity and distinction which it would never have possessed if by chance men had not built that spire precisely where it stands. This is not the case at Salisbury: I go out and away from the town and gaze at it from different points, and still see nothing but a spire, which, merely as a spire, may be the finest thing in the world, but is in no way related to the scene amidst which it is placed. We admire Salisbury just as we admire St. Paul's, for itself alone: it receives nothing from, and gives nothing to, nature: it is a gem of great value that would look just as well in any other setting. When I view the Chichester spire, it is but as a part of the scene—of all that visible nature that inspires in us feelings compared with which the highest pleasure the best and most perfect works of art can give is but a poor insipid thing, and as dreams compared to realities.

It is not, however, from all points of view that the Chichester spire is of so much account in the landscape. The line of the downs must appear beyond it; and downs and spire look best from the green level land between the cathedral and the sea. In some states of the weather the spire has a singular beauty, as when sun-flushed, it appears white against a black cloud. Perhaps the most beautiful effect is an afternoon or evening one, when there are clouds, but in the east and north a pale clear sky, against which the grey spire and distant downs appear sharply outlined; the earth green, but the hills in shadow deepest indigo blue. This effect is a very common one in autumn and winter evenings.

CHAPTER XIV

CHICHESTER

Chichester at a distance and near—Smells and sights—
Public-house signs—Habits of the people—Brewers'
policy—The church and the clergy—In the cathedral—A
wood-carving—Market-day—Early   associations—The
Market Cross and a mystery—Visit to Midhurst—Decaying
inns—Increase of temperance and the cause—Chichester
mud—Caging owls—The owl at Alfriston—A miserable
daw—A white owl's *He du Diable*—An ideal home for an
owl—A prisoner without hope.

To those who know not Chichester, that same tall, star-pointing spire
in a green level land with round blue hills beyond, is not only a thing
of beauty, a symbol and remembrancer; but seen at a distance, day
by day, from many points, may come to be even more than all these
to the mind. An ancient town, remote and rural; the sights and
sounds and quietude of nature, as in a village, around and in it,
where men may lead cleaner, saner, less strenuous lives than in the
great centres of population, and have other and better ideals.

But it is not so; for Chichester is not in itself sacred, nor pleasant, nor
fragrant to the nostrils. On the contrary, I am here always conscious
of an odour not easily described. Perhaps it comes nearest in
character to an effluvium ascending in warm and damp weather
from long-covered old forgotten cesspools, mixed with something
more subtle or volatile, like a fragrance that has lost its pleasantness.
It may be musk, with which the town dames perfumed themselves
in bygone centuries, still clinging to the old spot; and it may be the
ghost of old incense, which filled the sacred buildings every day for
ages before its ceremonial use was discontinued. This odour, or this
mixture of smells, of which the natives are not conscious, and the
sights which meet the eye, have in my case a profoundly depressing
effect. This depression is probably the malady commonly known as
"the chichesters, " from which many persons who visit this town are
said to suffer.

As to the sights: when you enter and walk in the streets, you
encounter a strange procession of signs, advancing to meet you, not
always singly, but often in twos and threes. They are implements of

husbandry, arms of all colours and degrees, castles, railways, telegraphs, globes, ships, tuns, anchors, crosses, and all sorts of objects. Products of the earth, too, are there, and signs that have rural associations—barley mows, wheat-sheafs, chestnuts, oaks, bushes, etc., etc. These are followed by creatures, wild and domestic, outlandish and familiar, real and fabulous—the most wonderful happy family on the globe. Behind a lively unicorn, run, trot, and prance a number of horses of all colours, and after these, white harts; then cows, spotted and red, and dogs, and bulls, and lambs, and swans, and eagles, and after them all a playful dolphin. Nor is this all; to the procession of birds and beasts and fishes, succeed things great and beautiful and magnificent—fountains and rainbows, and the sun in his glory, and the rising sun, and the moon and half-moon, and doubtless many stars and constellations; and angels, too, and beautiful thoughts and emotions, good intents, and hope, and I daresay faith and charity to keep her company.

These, the reader will understand, are public-house signs and names. They are symbols and descriptions not of things in nature and the soul, but of something better and dearer to the Chiches-terians, and their chief good. As to beauty in the moral or material world—

The bubbles that swim
On the beaker's brim
And break on the lips while meeting

is the most beautiful sight they know, and their joy for ever.

The amazing sight of all these signs, and other sights that are happily rare in small rural towns, led me to make a few inquiries, and the result may interest those of my readers who care to hear something (not too much) about the little ways and vagaries of their own species.

There are 12,000 souls in the town; that is to say, an adult male population of 3000. This number includes a rather large body of clergymen and ministers, and perhaps a couple of hundred highly respectable persons who do not go to bars. To provide this village population with drink there are seventy public-houses, besides several wine and spirit merchants, and grocers with licences. To keep all these houses open, all these taps perpetually running, there must be an immense quantity of liquor consumed. At eight o'clock in the morning you will find men at all the bars, often in groups of three or four or half a dozen, standing, pipe in mouth and tankard in hand; and at eleven at night, when closing-time comes, out of every door a goodly crowd of citizens are seen stumbling forth, surprised and sorry, no doubt, that the day has ended so soon. In the streets, near the railway station, at the Market Cross, and at various corners, you will see groups of the most utterly drink-degraded wretches it is possible to find anywhere in the kingdom—men with soulless bloated faces and watery eyes, dressed like tramps—standing idle with their hands in their pockets. But there is not a penny there, or they would not be standing in the mud and rain; and as for doing any work, they are past that. Here that rare spectacle, a man without a shirt, has met my sight, not once nor twice, but several times, the naked flesh showing through the rents of a ragged jacket buttoned or pinned up to the neck. These loathly human objects are strangely incongruous at that spot, under the great spire, in sight of the green open healthy downs, in perhaps the richest agricultural district in England.

But, it may be said, even allowing that every adult male in Chichester drinks every day, and drinks deeply, also allowing for market-day, when farmers and others who come into the town on business no doubt consume a good deal of beer and spirits, how is it possible for so many licensed houses to exist?

The publicans themselves told me how it was managed. They assert, and complain bitterly, that there are thirty or forty licensed houses too many in Chichester, and that if they had to pay anything approaching to the rents paid for houses of this description in other towns they could not live. Fortunately (and this is the silver lining to the poor publican's cloud) the rents are nominal, and in very many instances the houses are rent-free. The brewers own them, and find it more to their profit to give the house rent-free than to close it. The brewers, in fact, pay a heavy premium to the drink-sellers, lest any of their seventy precious licences should be lost.

As there are some extremists about just now, it is perhaps as well to say that I do not agree with them; and that, though not so enthusiastic as a clerical acquaintance of mine, who assures me that he "simply adores gin, " I am by no means an abstainer. Wine is among the kindly fruits of the earth which I appreciate, and failing that I can drink either ale or stout, or a mixture of both. But the perpetual swilling in Chichester is enough to turn the stomach of even the most tolerant man.

And the clergy and ministers of the gospel—there are, besides the cathedral, at least twenty churches and chapels in this small town—what are they doing in the matter? Nothing, I fear, and probably they have long discovered that nothing is to be done. The churches open on Sundays at an hour when the seventy public-houses are closed, and a certain number of women and a few married men attend the services. The cathedral has at least two services every day, and you will as a rule find six or eight to a dozen persons at the afternoon service; and these few are women, or strangers who have come in to look at the building. The eloquence, if there is any, the lessons, the sweet and beautiful voices singing "anthems clear, " are all wasted on the desert breath of that vast, vacant interior. The ghostly men walk the town like ghosts indeed, and are unseen or unnoticed, and at an immeasurable distance from the people they brush against; and they are like pilgrims and passengers in the city, whom nobody knows; nor does anyone inquire who they are, and what they are doing there.

On a rainy miserable day that was market-day, when the wind was cold and the streets were foul with mud; and the bellowings, bleatings, and grunt-ings of the animals, and the smell of the same, filled the air, I, greatly suffering from "the chichesters, " fled into the cathedral and broke my resolution never to enter that interesting part of the interior from which the non-paying public, the poor undistinguished herd of which I am a member, are excluded. I paid my coin and signed my name, and was one of a small exploring party of persons, damp and depressed as myself, under the guidance of a sexton or verger. He, unlike us, was in a rather merry mood, and gave a humorous colour to old traditions and historical incidents. When we had duly cursed Cromwell the Destroyer, as I daresay we had cursed him in many another noble building and in many a ruin, we came in our rambles to an ancient small chapel where we saw some curious old monkish wood-carvings which the Puritans ought in consistency to have destroyed, but did not. Here were oak seats in rows, and on the back of each one was a carving representing some humorous, fanciful, or grotesque scene, but I looked attentively at only one, the first that caught my eye. In this, a fox sat at ease in a chair, his legs crossed, his brush thrown carelessly like a long coat-tail across his lap, a stringed instrument on which he was merrily playing in his hand; his foot was pressed on the bosom of a goose, lying, poor wretch, screaming and flapping its wings at his feet; while he, inclining his sharp nose a little, was looking down much amused at the struggles of his victim. Opposite to him, in another chair, sat an ape, listening to the performance with all the gravity in the world.

Perhaps, thought I, those harsh and gloomy-minded men, who, in their zeal for their unlovely religion, destroyed so many works that had been a joy to men for centuries, had after all some sense of humour; and, with swords to hack in their hands, relented when they looked at this wicked and most comical fox.

I was still occupied with this carving when some person threw open a door, and called excitedly to our guide that a drove of pigs had broken or got into the cathedral grounds, and he was wanted at once to help get them out.

"I am not surprised, " I remarked. "The whole town swarms with pigs. " "Market-day! " he cried, and, apologising for leaving us so unceremoniously, he rushed away to give the assistance required.

I followed and gained the street, then took shelter from the driving rain under the ancient famous Market Cross, a richly-decorated stone pavilion, with many empty niches from which the stone effigies of great men were thrown down and shattered by the destructive Cromwellians.

This structure stands at the meeting of four streets—East, West, South, and North Streets. Formerly the cattle-market was held at this spot, and the narrow busy thoroughfares were then filled with cattle, sheep, and pigs, and of people buying and selling. A woman in a shop close by told me that about thirty years ago, when she was a child, the calves were always penned in the street directly before the house where she lived with her parents. The calves were brought in the day before market-day; and all night long, and a great part of the next day, the distressful lowings of the poor beasts sounded through the house; and so great was the effect on her, that up to the present time, after so many years, she cannot hear a calf calling without experiencing a sudden sense of misery and desolation, which is torture to her mind. So vivid are the impressions received, and so lasting the associations formed, pleasant and painful, in a child's mind! These seemingly trivial associations have a subtle influence, and are part of the character, a harmony or a discord according to their nature; and altogether they count for much in the little obscure history and tragedy of each individual life.

But we are now under the Market Cross.

If a stranger in the town, coming out of the empty desolate cathedral at the end of the afternoon service, should take refuge from the rain under its arches, he will presently see there a small, wizened, grey, threadbare ghost of a man, and probably take no notice of him. But if he, the stranger, with the confused sound of prayer and praise in that sacred empty building still in his ears, and a vague feeling of wonder and curiosity in his mind, should by chance fix his eyes on that small, faded, expressionless face, its colourless orbs will meet his, and he will read in them a vague response, an unshaped answer to his unshaped questions; and, by-and-by, the mysterious man, with a slight nod of invitation, will pass out, and the stranger, anxious to get to the bottom of the mystery, will follow. He will be led into I know not which of the four ways—North, South, East, or West; but close by, in one of them, his guide will pause, look back, then lightly run down a flight of narrow crooked stairs leading to a cellar. Following, the stranger will find himself in a dim, silent, crypt-like place, smelling of ancient damp and mould, dark at first to his unaccustomed eyes. But in a little while he will discern a huge recumbent form, paler in colour than the floor of rotting wood, the dripping stone walls, and vaulted roof—a stupendous human-shaped monster, like a Daniel Lambert increased to ten times his great size; his naked body and limbs extended on the black wet floor, apparently dead and swollen by death, but the head raised, supported by a hand and arm; the face, round as an ancient warrior's shield, but larger, turned to him, froth and yellow slime dropping from the obscene mouth, the wide bloodshot eyes fixed with a challenging gaze on his. Fascinated by that gaze, he, wide-eyed too, will stare back, even as a crystal-gazer looks expectant into a glass globe before him; and in those pale blue watery orbs he will see visions appearing and vanishing like lightning, an inconceivably rapid succession of faces, forms, events—wrecked lives of innumerable men, broken hearts and homes made desolate; famine and every foul disease; feverish dreams and appetites, frantic passions, crimes, ravings of delirium, epilepsy, insanity; and strewn over all, the ashes of death—all seen in one briefest moment of time.

Amazed and terrified at the sight of such things, he will turn and hurry away from that dreadful presence, a sudden darkness in his heart as if all the light and sweetness and glory had gone out of the world, all hope from the soul. And his guide will no longer be there; nor will he miss him, nor require to be told that he has been face to face with a god, the only god known and worshipped by the people of this town.

To come back. We have always known, since Cowper lived and was once near Chichester, that "man made the town, " and that he did not well make it, seeing that all vices and unhealthy appetites and habits and modes flourish most and take a darker colour in its close atmosphere. This being true of all towns, the only fair way to judge the moral state of any one town is to compare it with others, or with one other, not greatly differing from it in population, pursuits, and other conditions. Here, then, is an experience which seemed to me to throw a pretty strong light on the comparative position, with regard to the drinking habits of the people, of the cathedral town of Sussex.

From this agricultural centre, with a tall spire and many tavern signs to distinguish it, I went to Midhurst, on the other side of the downs, to find myself in a small, old, and extremely picturesque town, which, in its rough-paved, crooked, uneven streets, ancient timbered houses, its curfew bell, and darkness and silence at night, seemed to have suddenly carried me back into mediaeval times. But in spite of its hoary aspect and air of antiquity and remoteness and the number of inns, some very large, clustering about the central part, I felt as I wandered aimlessly about, and talked, when a chance offered, to working-men and with cottage women and children, that I had come into a different and better moral atmosphere. The inns appeared mostly empty, or doing nothing, and wore a neglected and decaying appearance. At night I went forth to explore, and stumbling along on the broken, up-and-down pavements, in a darkness made visible by a few widely-separated street lamps, I noticed that there were no lights, or nothing but a faint glimmer, in the windows of the inns and taverns. Finally, I made my way to a house which I had noticed and admired by daylight, taking it from its size and general appearance to be the oldest and most important inn or hotel in the town. After trying two or three doors, I found one that was not locked, and groped my way into a dim passage. To my summons a woman came with a candle, and led me into a large, dark, fireless room, and explained that there were no lights or fires in the parlours because no callers had been expected that evening. I declined to sit down in that cold, cheerless place, and, after some hesitation, she took me to an inner private room, where the landlord was sitting before a big fire. The room was exceedingly dirty, the floor littered with rubbish, and two or three days' ashes and cinders heaped in the fireplace; but it was warm, and light, and social. The landlord was eating his supper; he had it on the extreme corner of the clothless deal table, and it consisted of bread and cheese and raw onions. The room was full of the odour. I sat down on the other side of the fire; and there, in the innermost domestic circle, the so-to-speak fragrant bosom of the family, we had a good hour's talk, chiefly on the decline of the public business in Midhurst—a melancholy subject. I learnt that formerly there were more public-houses in the town, but some had been compelled to close, and that others were given by the owners, the brewers, rent free. My host paid not one penny rent for the grand old house he occupied, and even so he could hardly make a decent living out of it. Certainly his evening meal had not struck me as too luxurious and expensive. Another tenant of an ancient house close by was in even a worse case. This landlord, to make both ends meet and save the house, had conceived the happy idea of providing sleeping accommodation to poor vagrants at fourpence a night. He had gone into the byways and hedges for his guests, and his house had become well known to all the tramps and beggars that infest that part of Sussex. The ragged, verminous person who "begs your pardon" and wishes to say a word to you, is a common object in Midhurst or the neighbourhood. The word he wishes to say is that he is in want of just one penny to make up the sum of fourpence to pay for a bed at the hotel. A Midhurst man, a moderate drinker, with whom I had some conversation, told me that he had been all his life in the town, and that a great improvement in the drinking habits of the people had come about during the last twenty years. Notwithstanding that the population had been increasing, and a good deal of building going on, some of the old inns had been given up and no new ones had been opened, while others still open were in the degraded bankrupt state of those I have described. The brewers were probably not making anything out of houses kept up in this way; such houses may even be a loss to them, but being capitalists they can afford to hold on and wait for better times. A glorious wave of drunkenness may yet be witnessed in the land. The improvement noted had thus been brought about in spite of all that the brewers and their zealous and faithful friends and helpers, the licensing authorities, had been able to do to prevent it.

My interlocutor's belief was that this better state of things had resulted from the Education Act. Lads and young men now had interests, amusements, and ways of passing their leisure time which did not exist for their fathers. Newspapers and periodicals to read; cheap non-intoxicating drinks, and tea and coffee when wanted; indoor games, and field sports, the love of which is fostered at school, have served to make them independent of the tavern for amusement. I think it may be added that cigarette-smoking, which has become universal among the young people in the rural districts during the last five or six years, has been a blessing, too. It is true that in itself it is an evil, but a very mild one compared with the foul pipe of strong shag which the young men and youths of the peasant class used to smoke, and which is an incentive to beer-drinking.

Refreshed and exhilarated at what I had heard and seen at Midhurst, I went on my way, and before going many miles arrived at a place where there was a man who was a large employer of labour. I was assured that he would not employ a man from Mid-hurst on account of the well-known drunken habits of the people of that town!

What then shall we say of the cathedral town, which has lost none of its beer-houses, where doors are not closed and windows darkened at eight o'clock because it is not expected that anyone will call; where the brewers and their good friends, the licensing authorities, are determined that when a man staggers out of one tavern he shall not be obliged to walk more than twenty yards before finding another, where he may go in to quench his thirst?

But we have now happily done with this town and this subject. On many a wet day in autumn and winter, when walking in the streets and roads, I looked attentively at the mud, attracted by its peculiar grey colour; but I had no scientific person at my elbow to tell me about that soil and explain the cause of its pallid hue. Left to my own imaginings, I considered that Chichester was very old, that it was no doubt a walled town, perhaps very ancient, before Christ came, and that countless "generations of deciduous men" had fallen, to mix their ashes with the soil until it had in time taken that greyish colour. It was a comfort to reflect that if we cannot have anything in human shape better than "these common men, " now in the place of the vanished and forgotten, that these too will in a little while fade and fail and mix with and still further enrich the earth; and that out of a soil so fertilised, other brighter, higher forms and intelligences will eventually spring to life to make glad the world.

Before departing, never to return, I stepped aside from the road, and very carefully wiped the ash-coloured mud from my boots on the wet grass, for I wished not to take any of it away.

That was to me a sad day when I left, for I had but just come to the finish of a fight which I had been waging for some days, in which I had been finally worsted; and my only consolation in defeat was that it was in Chichester and not in any other town known to me in which the incident had occurred.

I have a great regard for the owl; the white owl, sometimes called the domestic owl, being a special favourite; and it greatly excites my indignation to see this bird in captivity. There is no reason, no excuse to be made, for confining him; he does not sing and twitter, nor amuse his gaoler with lively motions and brilliant colour. Beautiful to see when flying at sunset about the village and farm where he is not persecuted, and grotesque beyond description when viewed by day in his dimly-lighted loft or tower, rocking his body to and fro, now crouching cat-like, then stretching himself up, and all the time making strange weird faces at you, in a cage he is a most pitiful spectacle, a depressed, dead-alive-looking white owl, no longer white, his beautiful plumage smirched and disarranged.

  A robin redbreast in a cage
  Puts all heaven in a rage,

said Blake; and a white owl in a cage must produce the same effect, if we may indeed believe that unearthly eyes regard us, and see the fantastic tricks which we play with our unhappy fellow-creatures.

On one occasion only have I seen a caged owl without disgust and anger; this, oddly enough, was in downland, and the reader if, or when, he is in that part of the country, may see the bird for himself, and admire it as I did. It was at Alfriston, the ancient interesting village among the South Downs; and the bird was not the white nor any British owl, but an exceedingly fine specimen of the beautiful Cape horned owl. It is owned by an old dame, Mrs. Bodle, who keeps a very small sweet-stuff, orange, bun and lemonade shop in the village street. It was picked up, a young injured bird, by Mrs. Bodle's son, a soldier in South Africa, about seventeen years ago, and sent as a gift to his mother far away in the downland village. She has indeed cherished and kept it well, and loves it for itself as well as for her long-absent son's sake; very proudly she told me that many who had seen had wished to possess it, and had offered her a big price for her bird. Now the fame of the owl has spread; and all summer long, when visitors to the ancient village from Eastbourne, Seaford, Brighton, and other coast towns, are perpetually coming, many of them find their way to the little shop; and Mrs. Bodle does a good business and must be making a nice little fortune, and imagines (good soul!) that her ginger pop is more refreshing, her oranges and chocolates sweeter, and her buns more sustaining than those that others sell. But it is a delusion: most of those who eat her sweets and drink her lemonade go to see the bird, who sits all day (at the receipt of custom) in his big cage in a dim corner; strange and beautiful to look at in his rich, golden, tawny plumage, barred and mottled like a tiger-cat, with round, luminous, orange-coloured eyes, and the weird ornament of two large black ears. Mrs. Bodle informed me that he had a beautiful voice, but that he would only sing to or talk with her; on all others he looked gravely out of his brilliant orbs, but made no sound. However, after a little persuasion we got him to talk to us, and the note repeated again and again was like the cooing of a dove, but more musical; it was a softer, mellower, and more human sound than the hoot of the wood-owl.

Very different was the life of the white owl in Chichester. At the inn where I stayed on my last visit, I found three unhappy prisoners; two of these, a jackdaw and a blackbird, were kept in rabbit-hutch-like cages fixed against the ceiling of a long, narrow, dimly-lighted passage. It was sad to see the poor daw, the bird that loves soaring in wind and sunshine, shut up in that narrow house in a perpetual twilight, his head, when he sat on his perch, pressed against the ceiling. He always perched at the same end of his hutch, and the constant pressure of his head on one spot had made a hole in the plaster above. People were passing and repassing through that passage all day long, but without noticing the daw; for he was hung above the line, so to say, and to see him it was necessary to look up. Now, I observed that whenever I paused before the cage and looked up, the bird would instantly jump on to his perch, and, turning his back to me, fix his head against the ceiling in the corner, and remain motionless in that strange position. A silent, sullen daw—and no wonder! He did not, like Sterne's captive starling, cry continually, "I can't get out"; he made no cry, and had no hope of ever feeling the wind and the sun, or ever seeing the blue sky and green earth again. Eight to nine years had he been immured in that cursed prison, and he would never leave it until his tortured life had left him; then his dead body would be taken out, and another bird, I daresay, put there in his place.

The third prisoner was the owl, and I think he was even worse off than the others; for he was kept in an always malodorous and usually uncovered cage, in the kitchen, where a big fire was burning sixteen to seventeen hours every day. The heat must have been—and alas! still must be—dreadful to the poor bird; but if speech had been given him he would, I think, have complained most of the gas jets: they were burning all about him until twelve o'clock every night, and the sensation they produced must have been as of fine heated needles, heated red and heated white, stabbing and pricking his sensitive eye-balls. In this chamber of torture the miserable bird had existed for nine months.

When I went to the landlady to plead for the owl, I was very diplomatic, remembering what certain wise men have taught us— namely, that if we want to get anything out of anybody we must not begin by rubbing him up the wrong way. I praised her greatly for her merciful heart, and told her how it had delighted me to hear her fame in Chichester as a lover and protector of animals. But her treatment of her feathered pets was wrong; and in mild language I imparted my views on the subject. She was disturbed at what I said about the owl, and began to excuse herself, saying that she had taken in the bird solely to give it a safe and happy home, but she had no desire to keep it as it was a silent dull bird, and that if I wished I could take it away and set it free.

I was delighted at my success, and promised to find before long a suitable home for the bird.

For some days after that I kept a look-out during my rambles; and one afternoon, in the maritime district, I came to a small village which struck me as an ideal home for an owl. For it was a small and most rustic place, consisting of a little church and a great thatched barn and many farm buildings. But the farm-house itself, even in this land of great old farms that were once manors, was a surprise to me. It was a very large low stone building, partly overgrown with ivy, and nearly surrounded by an ancient foss, with great old elm trees growing out of the banks. The people who lived in this grey old manse were worthy of their home: the lady of the house, who received me, was young and fair to see, and gracious in mind and manner; and when I told her my errand, she said that she and her husband were very fond of birds and had a peculiar regard for the white owl; and that if I would take and release it in their barn she herself would place food for it there every day and see that it was not disturbed, until it had recovered its strength and the use of its wings and could find its own living. Meanwhile my landlady had changed her mind, and when I was ready to take the bird she informed me that she had decided not to part with it; that on thinking the matter over she had found out that she had become attached to the owl, and she also thought that the bird would be unhappy if taken from the home and the surroundings he was accustomed to.

In vain I begged and pleaded, not that day only, but the next, and for several days. She would not part with the bird for love or money. Up till then I had visited the bird every day, and opening its cage would put my hand in to caress it. It liked to be gently stroked on the breast, and when caressed in this way would play with my fingers, biting them but very gently with his beak. But from that time I was ashamed to go near him, or even to look at him; for I had promised him his liberty, and could not keep my word. Nor was it necessary that I should look at to see him; his melancholy image was too deeply graved in my mind—a feathered Dreyfus, Semitic features and all, the head bowed, the weary eyes closed, the hooked nose just visible amidst a wilderness of white whiskers. I could only try to believe that there is some foundation for the ancient belief held in so many lands, that the owl is indeed a supernatural, or sacred, bird; that when this captive had been tortured to death and its carcass thrown into the dust-heap, the loving kindness that had been shown to him would have a swift and suitable reward.

CHAPTER XV

WINTER IN WEST DOWNLAND

A good-bye to towns—Charm of West Downland in winter—A cow-boy singing and a missel-thrush—A vein of stupidity—Anecdotes—Bats eating bacon—Riding to Ringmer and a downland man's ignorance—Chilgrove—Gilbert White—Yew, juniper, and clematis—A wooded combe—A host of wood-pigeons—Beautiful downland scenery—Fallen beech-leaves on snow—South Harting—Conclusion.

It would not be appropriate, nor even seemly, that a book of this sort, treating of rural scenes and wild life, in which, while keeping a vigilant eye on what my pen was doing, I have yet allowed it to hint or suggest, in a few faintly-traced lines, what communion with nature really is to me—it would not be proper that it should conclude with an account of any town, and the writer's adventures, the thoughts and experiences that afflicted him, during his sojourn in it.

A friend of mine, a downland rector, expressed his disappointment at finding that this book was not what he had thought it was intended to be—a Flora of the South Downs. It was true, he said, that plants had not interested him, and that the only wild flowers he could give a name to when he saw them were the daisy and dandelion; still it would have been a satisfaction to have a Flora of the downs on his bookshelves for reference; and that was what he had looked for, instead of this—well—this sort of thing.

As a fact, there are several printed lists of the downland plants to be had by those who want them; and doubtless there are scores of men and women who would be only too delighted to compile more such lists—as many lists, manuals, floras, in fact, as the publishers and the public would like to buy. Had I written a book of that kind, instead of "this sort of thing, " I should not have been able to say anything about the smells of Chichester, material and moral, which are in no way related to flowers.

It cannot be said of other downland towns that they are inodorous, or sweet, or flowery; they are not that: we all know of *loud* smells, the metaphor being common, and coming down to Brighton with senses purified and sharpened by the mountain air one is hailed and assailed by perfect trumpet-blasts from the innumerable fried-fish shops that flourish in that watering-place. The smells of the cathedral town are not of this pronounced and vulgar description; they are subtle, mysterious, but unhappily they cling longer to the mind.

No; it was better in the end, or before the end, to escape from that atmosphere out into the fresh world; to be blown through and through by the winter gale, until that effluvium, and all memory of it, had been blown out of my nostrils and soul; to be washed clean by the lustral water of the rain, sparkling silvery and crystal as it fell, and the wind-chased snow-flakes that first whitened and then melted on me—to be one with nature, purified and myself once more.

Better days than those spent in roughest weather on the hills I could not well have known. "Oh, but you should visit this part of downland in spring! " I was told again and again. It was good enough in mid-winter in spite of weather of the kind we call bad; so good indeed as to make me somewhat sceptical as to its far greater attractiveness in summer. Is there anything in rural England more gratifying to the eye than a winter prospect in this green diversified country, with leafless beechen woods spread over slopes and summits, and gathered like darkest purple clouds within the combes and hollows of the great round hills!

Glad as I was to be out in wind and rain and snow on the summits, it was often a relief to escape from so furious a blast by going down to the sheltered weald, the flat, wooded country between Mid-hurst and Harting, where I loved to walk, and where these rambles had to end. I walked by the Rother, that fairest Sussex river, among the brown and purple woods, and darker pine. Walking there one day about noon, when the sky was a very soft blue, with a few fleecy grey clouds floating in it, and the wind was still, I came to a wide heath somewhere between Midhurst and Trotton. It was very silent; only two sounds were audible, and I stood for some time listening to them. One was the sound of a boy singing. He was a cow-boy; I could see him out in the middle of the heath, standing among the furze-bushes, where his cows were grazing. He was perhaps a choir-boy in one of the village churches; at all events, he was singing a hymn in a trained and very beautiful voice. In that still, open air, at the distance I heard him (two to three hundred yards), the voice seemed purer and sweeter than any boy's voice I have ever heard in any church or cathedral. No doubt it was the distance, the silence of nature, the wild, solitary scene, and perhaps, too, the abundant moisture in the air, that gave the voice its exceeding beauty; and the effect was as if this sound, too, had been cleansed and clarified by the rains, even as the sky had been washed to that softest, lucid blue. I listened to the boy singing and singing, with a short interval after each verse, and to the one other sound, which came to me from an equal distance on the opposite side—the singing of a solitary missel-thrush. The clear, bell-like note of the bird filled the intervals in the boy's singing; and the bird, like the boy, had a clearer, purer voice on that day; and like the other, too, he sang verse after verse, with short intervals between. The effect was indescribably beautiful. At last I thought I would go and make the boy's acquaintance. Many a little fellow tending cows on a heath have I talked with, and this one had something more in him than all those I had known. As I went over the rain-sodden heath, often getting into hidden water, the singing ceased, and when I had got to where the cows were feeding among some large furze-bushes the boy was not there, or at all events not visible. I had seen his grey cap as he watched my approach from behind a bush a few minutes before; but he was not there now; he had concealed himself like a shy little lizard, or furze wren, and after looking about among the bushes for some minutes, I gave it up.

Possibly it was nothing more than a little rustic's shyness that had made him hide; but it is a fact, I think, that there is a streak or vein of stupidity, which, running eastward from Hampshire, crops up in many places among the West Sussex downs.

One day, seeing a youth harnessing a pony at a gate, I asked him the name of a hill over which I had just walked. "I don't know, " he returned, evidently surprised at the question; "I never heard that it had a name. " A hill, I assured him, must have a name; and I remarked that he was probably new to the neighbourhood. He assured me that he was a native of the place, and that to his knowledge the hill had no name; then he added casually, "We call it Bepton Hill. "

A day or two later a man told me of an inn, away from any road, in a deep wooded valley among the hills, where I could get refreshment, and he was very particular about giving me proper directions. "What is the name of the inn? " I asked, and he replied that it had no name. "An inn, " I said, "must have a name—it is not like a hill that can do without one. " He shook his head. "We call it the Oak, " he remarked finally; "but if it has a name I never heard it, and I have known the place a good many years now. "

I might have been among the aborigines of Venezuela, or of some other wild remote land, where every person and perhaps every place has a real name which is a secret known to few, and sometimes to nobody; and an appellation besides which is not a real name, but a sort of nickname, or false or common name, by which he or she or it is called.

Amusing instances of ignorance, too, and of old erroneous beliefs which have died out in most places, are commonly met with in this out-of-the-way corner of Sussex. One spring-like evening in January, when talking with some working-men at the village of Lavant, I called their attention to a bat flying to and fro near us as a proof of the mildness of the weather.

"You call it a bat, " said one man, "and I grant it's very like one; but I call it a fluttermouse. You see it's bigger than a bat; but they are all of one specie. The bigger ones, the fluttermouses as we calls them, are the ones that eats the bacon. They comes down the chimney to get it, when it's hanging there to smoke. " I tried to convince him that he was blaming the wrong animal, but he stuck to it that it was the fluttermouses and not the mouses that stole the bacon, and finally asserted that he had actually seen them at it.

About this matter Gilbert White remarks, "The notion that bats go down chimneys and gnaw men's bacon, seems no improbable story." This reference to White has served to remind me that one of the most surprising instances of ignorance I have met with in the downs was in an educated man.

Readers of the Selborne Letters are familiar with the name of Ringmer, the pretty, old Sussex village in the neighbourhood of Lewes whither the famous naturalist used to make an annual journey on horseback. His visits were to his aunt Rebecca, the wife of Henry Snooke, and the house they lived in is still standing. The egregious Mr. Augustus Hare, in his *Sussex*, speaking of Ringmer, reminds his readers that it was from this village that White dated "several of his stilted letters. "

During the summer of 1898, in the course of a ramble on the downs, I made the acquaintance of a gentleman who is a native, and had spent the sixty odd years of his life in those parts. Both the man and the name he bore interested me, the name being a peculiar and a very ancient one at that spot. The family is now impoverished and decayed, but there was little sign of decay in my casual acquaintance, despite his years. A straight wiry man, with alert hawk-like eyes, extremely active in his habits, a field naturalist in a way, devoted to sport, and an excellent judge of the points of a horse or dog. He also had some acquaintance with books, and took an interest in most things; above all things he was interested in his own beloved South Downs, and he maintained that for a man who preferred an outdoor life, and the freedom of an unenclosed country and of great hills, there was no spot on the globe to compare with it.

In the course of a conversation I had with him after we had known each other a few days and were becoming fairly intimate, he spoke two or three times of his rides to Ringmer. At length, with a laugh, I said that he reminded me of Gilbert White, who, although living far away in Hampshire, was also accustomed to ride to Ringmer. As he did not appear to understand my remark, I was compelled to explain that I was speaking of the Rev. Gilbert White, author of the *Natural History of Selborne*. Alas! I only made matters worse, since after ransacking his brain for some moments, he confessed that he had never heard the name of Gilbert White nor of the village of Selborne.

I was reminded of an experience I had on a steamboat in the Solent. It was many years ago, when I was a stranger in a strange land. I got into conversation with a gentleman on the deck, who lived on the island, and when near Cowes he gave me the names of several of the yachts we saw anchored there, and told me a good deal about their owners. He said that the island was now a favourite place of residence for men who had made a name in the world, and he proceeded to speak of several of these famous persons. I was a little ashamed to find that they were nearly all unknown to me. The greatest among them, judging from his way of speaking of him, was the editor of a sporting paper, who had built himself a house in the neighbourhood of Osborne.

I remarked that he had omitted all mention of one of the great men who lived on the island—Alfred Tennyson. "Who's he? " said my interlocutor. "A retired admiral? No! What has he done? —does he keep a yacht? "

I did not think he kept a yacht; and he had not done anything that I knew of except to write poetry: he was the poet-laureate.

"A poet! —I know nothing about poets, " he said a little curtly, and very soon afterwards walked off.

It is one of our commonest delusions that the balance in which we weigh our fellow-creatures, our measure and perspective, are those in use by mankind generally: very naturally it disgusted him to have my poor little obscure poet—all poets were little obscure people to his mind—brought into the distinguished company of sporting men who kept their yachts in the Solent! All that I could readily understand—my delusion was just as natural as, and not less laughable than his; but to meet with a gentleman who was naturalist as well as sportsman, who had spent all the years of his life on that "majestic chain of mountains called the South Downs, " and was accustomed to ride to Ringmer, yet was ignorant of the name of White of Selborne, filled me with astonishment and even humiliation.

About the house at Ringmer in which White spent so many of his autumns, the late Mark Antony Lower, the well-known and excellent writer on local subjects, relates that some years ago (the date is not given, but I believe it must have been about 1850) a gentleman who occupied it as tenant had all the nightingales frequenting the grounds destroyed. Their late singing disturbed his rest. A strange fate for the birds that "sing darkling, " the creatures of "ebullient heart, " to have met at such a spot! This irritable gentleman, like my downland friend, had never perhaps heard of the parson of Selborne; on the other hand, he had perhaps heard too much about him, and desired, after the fashion of the Stratfordian who cut down the sacred mulberry tree, to express his disapproval of the man or of his work. That his neighbours did not hunt him out of the village, or even gently remove him from a world in which he was manifestly out of place—"a harsh discordant thing"—does not show us the Ringmerites in too favourable a light.

There are many, memories of Gilbert White in this part of downland, as it was his custom when travelling to Ringmer to break his journey at Chil-grove, a charming spot among the downs about midway between Petersfield and Chichester, and at Shopwyke House, close to Chichester. Chilgrove Manor was owned by his friend, Mr. Woods, who gave White the information about the stone-curlews on the downs; and Shopwyke House was owned by another member of the Woods family, who was Gilbert White's relation by marriage. The present squire of Chilgrove is a grandson of White's friend. During my rambles in this part I paid two visits to Chilgrove House, which has been rebuilt since White's time, and retain very pleasant recollections of the kind and gracious members of the family I saw there.

But if there remains anything of interest to be said about White's intercourse with the Woods family and his connection with this part of Sussex, it will doubtless be told by my friend Dr. Bowdler Sharpe in the new edition of the *Letters* he is preparing for the press. We have lately had a good many editions of White; but this will be definitive—one which every British naturalist will feel obliged to add to his collection; and with this book, and the exhaustive Life lately contributed to the *Dictionary of National Biography* by Professor Alfred Newton, on our shelves, there will be, I imagine, a slackening of the hunt after fresh materials, since there can be but little left to reward even the most diligent gleaner.

In Chapter XII. I have said not a little about the arborescent vegetation characteristic of the West Sussex downs; and I trust the reader will pardon me if I go back to that subject here. At Chilgrove there is a wood which, seen at a distance, looks almost as uniformly dark as the famous yew grove at Kingly Bottom; but although the yew abounds greatly in it and the trees are well grown, throwing out immense horizontal branches near the ground, giving it that dark and sombre aspect, it is on a nearer view found to be composed of all the trees and bushes characteristic of the chalk downs—yew, beech, holly, thorn, juniper, furze, and wild clematis. It grows on the side, near the top, of a long, steep, hanger-like hill, and overhangs the Chilgrove vale. A wilder and more beautiful wood of that peculiar type found only among the West Sussex downs I had never seen. Most of it was an almost impenetrable thicket and tangle, and in the open spaces the foot sank deep in the thick growth of softest moss. Here were the largest furze and juniper bushes I have seen in Sussex, the junipers being, some of them, poplar-and cypress-shaped, and others with wide-spreading branches, looking like yews of a lively green. Some were fifteen to eighteen feet high, with a girth of two to three feet; and some of the yew-shaped bushes had branches six to eight feet in length. Here I observed that the great masses of black-green yew-tree foliage formed a wonderfully effective background to the feathery foliage of the juniper, a bright but very delicate glaucous green.

On the edge of this wood I found that curiosity in plant life—a perfect wild clematis tree. As a rule when a thorn tree, robbed of light and air by a too luxuriant clematis spread over it, perishes and finally crumbles to dust, the semi-parasite dies after it, being unable to keep itself up, or to live when prostrate on the earth. Occasionally, however, it does succeed in keeping off the ground for a time, but in most cases it has a widowed, forlorn appearance, swayed about this way and that on its too slender stem, its head bowed down, and the long attenuated twigs drooping like loosened hair to the earth. Here is a clematis that has a different aspect, with a round, straight, and shapely trunk, twenty-seven inches in circumference; its height is eighteen feet, and its innumerable fine pendulous branches give it the appearance of a weeping-willow tree. At the end of January when I saw it, it was still clothed in down as with a silver-grey fluffy foliage.

On the north escarpment of the downs, at this point, there are some fine yew groves and woods in the deep combes and hollows and ravine-like clefts in the sides of the hills. The finest of these is on the north side of the great down west of West Dean woods. Here, in the side of the hill, there is an immense basin-shaped combe, its sloping circular sides covered with a dense dark growth of yews, and under these, the flat bottom of the basin is filled with a beechen wood. Seated on the turf on the rim of this great hollow in the side of the hill, one evening in late January, I had beneath me a scene to make a man's heart glad. I had only just discovered this hidden wood, and it came as a complete surprise; nothing quite like it had I seen before. In summer, when the beeches would appear from above as a floor of deep uniform green, there would not perhaps have been any special beauty in this spot. Winter had given the charm and magical effect it had for me on that evening, when the sun was going down in a cold but very clear sky. For the tall beeches on which I looked down appeared as innumerable white or pale columns standing on a floor of red and russet gold, and white columns and golden floor were all the more beautiful for being seen through the almost cloud-like tracery of innumerable purple and purplish-red or "murrey"-coloured branchlets. The rich colour of that temple and palace of nature—the golden floor and purple roof—made the wide band of the yew wood seem black by contrast; and above the black yews the smooth turf of the hilltop looked a pale green.

One thing that added greatly to the charm of this wood was the vast multitude of wood-pigeons which were congregated in it. It was, I found, their favourite roosting-place in this neighbourhood. Alarmed at my presence they began to rush out of the trees on all sides in numbers, the sudden sharp clatter of their wings sounding at a distance like castanets. By-and-by they were all on the wing, gathered in one immense flock, rushing about this way and that in the vast wooded hollow beneath my feet, looking at times almost white as they streamed over the black yews and caught the level sunbeams on their upper plumage. This flock could not have numbered less than two to three thousand birds. Finally they began to settle on the beeches, and when all had settled, and with my powerful binocular I had brought them so close to me as to be able to see distinctly all the delicate shading of their plumage and the brighter colours of beak and eye, I had before me as fascinating a tree-and-bird scene as it is possible to imagine. The colour and grace of it could not be described—the multitude of birds, thick as starlings in the purple branches, not yet recovered from their alarm, but every one still moving its head and flirting its tail, and evidently anxious to keep an eye on the suspicious-looking (although gunless) intruder on their privacy.

Of all man's inventions, this is to me the most like a divine gift—this double tube in my hand, which enables me to follow the beautiful children of the air in their flight; and when they are at home and safe in woods, and on green waves, and on cliffs, to sit or float as it were invisible and unsuspected among them.

West of the wooded spots I have described in the neighbourhood of West Dean, the charm of this part of the downland country if anything increases; until, at Up Park and South Harting, when we are on the border of Hampshire, and can no further go, we are in the midst of the most beautiful scenery of the West Sussex downs.

At this point there are more woods and copses resembling in character those described, composed of yew, thorn, holly, juniper, and furze; but the large woods are mostly beech. In a former chapter I have described a singular and very pretty effect produced by fallen beech leaves blown in drifts against the juniper scrub on an open down. At Up Park again I saw another pretty scene caused by beech leaves carried to a distance by the wind. On the lower slope of a large smooth round down, covered with frozen snow, there was a beech wood, through which a violent north-east wind was blowing, lifting myriads of fallen leaves and driving them over the smooth hill. The scene reminded me of a great migration of butterflies, a phenomenon which I had witnessed on two occasions in a distant country. The travelling insects flew close to the surface, and their bright-red fluttering wings showed well against the green of the spring grass that covered the plain; but these innumerable fallen leaves, red and russet gold, in the winter sunshine, chased by the wind over that wide expanse of snow, produced an effect even more novel and beautiful.

The village of South Harting itself is not unworthy of its setting of green hills and purple woods: of all the downland villages it is to my mind the most attractive. It is, moreover, distinct and individual, without any resemblance to the others that one likes best—Alfriston, Jevington, West Dean (the village of that name on the Cuckmere), Wilmington, Berwick, Ditchling, and perhaps half a dozen more. Its attractiveness is partly due to its unrivalled situation, and in part to the materials of which it is built—a smooth cream-coloured stone dressed with red brick. The creamy-white stone, set off with the deep red of the door and window mouldings, and the corners of the walls, has a peculiarly soft and delicate appearance. Best of all, the church, rarely beautiful in itself, is in perfect harmony with its surroundings. It is a large, low building, cream-white and red like the houses and cottages, with an immense sloping red-tiled roof, stained with many-coloured lichen and adorned with the most graceful shingled spire to be seen in downland.

The church at Alfriston has been called the "Cathedral of the South Downs"; and from a historical and archaeological point of view, it may be the most important and interesting of the downland churches; for pure beauty it cannot compare with that of South Harting. The sight of a church like this, and the pleasure it gives, makes one almost weep to think of all the important churches one knows, built by the best architects, of the best materials, and at an enormous cost, which fail to please us, and are often even distressing to look at, all because they are out of place where they stand—out of keeping and out of harmony with every building and every object near them, and with the surrounding scenery.

An account of the last day but one spent by me at this pleasant spot will perhaps strike the reader as a not inappropriate ending of this chapter, and of the book. It was a spring-like day in mid-February (1900), a few miles from Harting, when, after dinner, I went out for a long walk with a man who was a native of the place. It is the rarest thing for me to have a companion out of doors: a day in the woods or any wild place with another is to me, in most cases, a wasted day. But with this man I went gladly; for although not an educated person, and no naturalist, there was that in him which made him to differ from the others of his class: in his way of thinking and mode of life he was somewhat apart. Besides, he badly wanted to show me something, and to tell me something. What he wanted to show me was the scenery amid which he had lived; and he took me a round of twelve or fourteen miles, in the course of which we came two or three times on the Rother and followed its windings for some distance; we also visited two or three pretty little rustic villages, and passed through several woods and copses, and up and down some hills, pausing from time to time to take in a particularly fine prospect.

These were the scenes familiar to him since his childhood, amidst which he had lived with a few intervals all his life. He told me that on three or four occasions he had left home to better himself, and had been absent from one to three years; but though he could make more money at a distance, and had more comforts, he had on each occasion felt himself compelled to return, and he had now definitely abandoned all idea of leaving his native place again. He was anxious to make me understand the character and strength of the feeling that always drew him back; and in a roundabout but singularly effective method he succeeded very well. It was not any human tie—it was the place. This, away from home, was his experience. When he was hungry he enjoyed his food, and when he was tired, rest was grateful. He slept well, and always after a night's rest felt refreshed and glad to begin the day's work, and his health always and everywhere was remarkably good. But it was all of no benefit: every feeling of comfort, of a want relieved, of satisfaction, of pleasure, was but for a moment; it passed and left him still wanting, wishing, waiting, for something else. It was like the feeling a traveller has who is anxious to get to the end of his journey. He might just as well have been out of health, or out of work and penniless—hungry, ill-clothed, and with an anxious mind. And on each occasion, when, on account of this perpetual gnawing dissatisfaction with life, he came back to the old place, instantly the trouble vanished; he breathed freely and was at rest once more, perfectly contented, perfectly happy.

It took him a long time to tell me all this, as he had some difficulty in putting his ideas into words; and then followed the declaration—a wholly false conclusion to which he had been brought—that the scenery in this corner of West Sussex, amid which he had lived and which he had shown me with so much pride, was the most perfectly beautiful in the whole country. For how else could it have taken such a hold upon his heart as to make it impossible for him to exist in any comfort away from it?

He was not overpleased to hear me say that he was mistaken; that the home feeling is in some degree universal in men born and bred amid rural scenes, but varies greatly in different persons; and that when it is exceptionally strong, as in his case, it produces an illusion and a delusion—a belief that the one loved spot is in itself in some way better than all other places; that the superior beauty, or charm, or restfulness which the heart finds in that spot is actually inherent in it. Much more I said on this subject, and told him that men had been known even to die of that malady that had affected him, although the scenes for which they had pined had not been distinguished by beauty or any peculiarly attractive quality above others.

I fancy that after all I did not convince him of his error. I rather hope not. For now when I recall the scenes we looked upon together—that wild stream of the Rother; the small old-world peaceful villages; the hills of so pure and fresh a green, their lower slopes and valleys purple and dark with beech and pine; when I find how persistently it all comes back to me, and how vivid and beautiful the impression is, I am not quite sure that I was wholly right in my philosophy, and that his delusion was nothing but a delusion.

THE END

Lightning Source UK Ltd.
Milton Keynes UK
27 December 2010

164890UK00001B/42/P

9 781409 905332